ASHE Higher Education Report: Volume 37, Number 5
Kelly Ward, Lisa E. Wolf-Wendel, Series Editors

Postsecondary Education for American Indian and Alaska Natives: Higher Education for Nation Building and Self-Determination

Bryan McKinley Jones Brayboy

Amy J. Fann

Angelina E. Castagno

Jessica A. Solyom

D1637429

Discover this journal online at
WILEY ONLINE LIBRARY
wileyonlinelibrary.com

76 999 1349

Postsecondary Education for American Indian and Alaska Natives: Higher Education for Nation Building and Self-Determination
Bryan McKinley Jones Brayboy, Amy J. Fann, Angelina E. Castagno, and Jessica A. Solyom
ASHE Higher Education Report: Volume 37, Number 5
Kelly Ward, Lisa E. Wolf-Wendel, Series Editors

ISSN 1551-6970   electronic ISSN 1554-6306   ISBN 978-1-1183-3883-4

The ASHE Higher Education Report is part of the Jossey-Bass Higher and Adult Education Series and is published six times a year by Wiley Subscription Services, Inc., A Wiley Company, at Jossey-Bass, One Montgomery Street, Suite 1200, San Francisco, California 94104-4594.

For subscription information, see the Back Issue/Subscription Order Form in the back of this volume.

CALL FOR PROPOSALS: Prospective authors are strongly encouraged to contact Kelly Ward (kaward@wsu.edu) or Lisa Wolf-Wendel (lwolf@ku.edu). See "About the ASHE Higher Education Report Series" in the back of this volume.

Visit the Jossey-Bass Web site at **www.josseybass.com.**

Printed in the United States of America on acid-free recycled paper.

The ASHE Higher Education Report is indexed in CIJE: Current Index to Journals in Education (ERIC), Education Index/Abstracts (H.W. Wilson), ERIC Database (Education Resources Information Center), Higher Education Abstracts (Claremont Graduate University), IBR & IBZ: International Bibliographies of Periodical Literature (K.G. Saur), and Resources in Education (ERIC).

Advisory Board

The ASHE Higher Education Report Series is sponsored by the Association for the Study of Higher Education (ASHE), which provides an editorial advisory board of ASHE members.

Contents

Executive Summary

American Indian and Alaska Native enrollment in higher education has more than doubled in the past thirty years, yet American Indian/Alaska Native (AI/AN) students continue to be significantly underrepresented in institutions of higher education and continue to face barriers that impede their academic success. This underrepresentation is troubling, given that many Indigenous students indicate having expectations of attending and graduating college from as early as elementary school. This monograph explores the state of higher education for American Indian and Alaska Native peoples in the United States. Beginning with an examination of the legacy of Western education in Indigenous communities and the experiences of Indigenous students in the K–12 system, we explore the factors that influence college going and, upon enrollment in institutions of higher education, the factors that influence college completion. From pre-K–16 to students in graduate programs, whether attending school in rural or urban settings, in mainstream or tribally controlled institutions, we explore the role of academic institutions and personnel, family and community, and tribal nations in student achievement. Additionally, we explore the experiences of AI/AN graduates in their transition from student to faculty. We conclude by offering a number of recommendations for how to improve the success of Indigenous students and faculty.

As we walk the reader through what we know about higher education for Indigenous students, we weave central themes of nation building, sovereignty, self-determination, Indigenous knowledge systems, as well as the role of culturally responsive teaching and learning throughout the discussion. We argue that the success of Indigenous students depends on institutional practices and tribal nation support; we also argue that attention to nation-building strategies is a vital part of academic success. Additionally, we believe institutions of higher education must address institutional-specific issues related to the recruitment, retention, and graduation, and that their efforts will be most successful if they become more knowledgeable about the unique experiences, expectations, and goals of Indigenous people(s) and nations. Conversely, Indigenous communities, families, and nations also play an important role in supporting and facilitating student success. Connections to ideas of sovereignty, self-determination, and nation building highlight potential paths and areas of strength for American Indian/Alaska Natives in institutions of higher education. We believe that there is, in fact, a role for higher education in Indigenous communities and nations.

The monograph is organized in the following manner: In the first chapter we present a cursory overview of the reasons for which Indigenous students and communities remain absent from the fabric of mainstream institutions of higher education.

The next chapter, "Framing the Conversation," builds on the recognition that Indigenous students often pursue higher education as a means to improve the myriad ways in which they can serve their families, communities, and tribal nations. The goal of serving to benefit and strengthen Indigenous communities is one part of the larger concept of nation building and is a fundamental part of this monograph. The concept of nation building is, in fact, the glue that binds together the data-driven chapters in the monograph. Drawing on the work of various disciplines and scholars, including Indigenous legal and education scholars such as David Wilkins, Duane Champagne, Jo-Ann Archibald, Marie Battiste, Rebecca Tsosie, Taiaike Alfred, and Vine Deloria, Jr., we explore the importance of Indigenous knowledge systems, tribal nation building, and culturally responsive schooling and their implications for American Indian success in institutions of higher education. The remaining chapters extend and apply the concepts introduced in this chapter.

A chapter entitled "Postsecondary Access for Indigenous Students" focuses on postsecondary access to higher education for Indigenous students. Issues of high school completion, achievement on standardized college entrance exams, and the role of schools and college counselors in developing a college-going culture among students at the K–12 level are explored in detail. Additionally, the influence of family and cultural practices in academic achievement are explored as sources of strength and support for Indigenous students.

"American Indian and Alaska Native College Students" looks specifically at the undergraduate experience for Indigenous students. We focus on enrollment patterns, particularly in terms of graduation and attrition rates, and explore the myriad factors that contribute to the success of Indigenous students in these settings in addition to the challenges faced.

The next two chapters discuss the postbaccalaureate experiences of Indigenous graduate students and faculty within postsecondary institutions. We present some of the unique challenges in these settings. We conclude by discussing the importance that persisting in these settings presents for Indigenous students and faculty members as well as the tribal communities they serve.

The final chapter presents a discussion about the policy, practice, and research implications of the discussions offered throughout the monograph. We focus on the implications for practices at multiple levels—ranging from the local/tribal, state, and federal level—and suggest that both educational institutions and tribal nations must consider the long-term effects past, existing, and future educational practices present for Indigenous students and the continued success of Indigenous communities.

A Note on Author Contributions

Any coauthored work requires input from multiple sources and different effort on parts of the text. We wanted to offer a brief note on the division of labor in this text in order to make explicit the ways that we each contributed to the writing of this text. All of the authors significantly contributed to the production of this text.

Bryan, Angelina, and Jessica originally drafted the introduction of the text, once the other chapters had been written. Amy authored a small portion of the introduction. Angelina, Jessica, and Bryan authored "Framing the Conversation." Bryan and Angelina, working with Jessica, wrote "American Indian and Alaska Native College Students." There are parts of the chapter that include Amy's work from another project; Bryan, Angelina and Jessica revised the original draft.

Amy authored "Postsecondary Access for Indigenous Students," "American Indian and Alaska Native Graduate Students," and "American Indian and Alaska Native Faculty." Jessica and Bryan assisted with literature searches for "American Indian and Alaska Native Faculty." Jessica, Angelina, and Bryan made the connections to nation building more evident in "Postsecondary Access for Indigenous Students," "American Indian and Alaska Native Graduate Students," and "American Indian and Alaska Native Faculty." All four authors worked to revise these chapters. Bryan, Angelina, and Jessica authored "Where Do We Go From Here?" Hints of the recommendations appeared in a policy report that Bryan published in 2007. Amy made additional connections to federal policies. At the end of the project, all four authors made minor (and in some cases substantive) revisions to the entire text.

Bryan, Angelina, and Jessica will donate all of their proceeds from this manuscript to assist American Indians and Alaska Natives in institutions of higher education.

Foreword

When colleges and universities talk about multiculturalism and diversity, there is a common assumption that all underrepresented groups are included. But, frequently and typically, American Indian and Alaskan Native students, faculty, and administrators are overlooked in these conversations because of their limited presence on most college campuses. They are also underrepresented in many studies and in most data sources (institutional and national). The "n" is often just too small for Native Americans to be counted or included in a meaningful way. When Native American populations are included or discussed it tends to be from a deficit perspective—they are least likely to earn degrees, graduate from high school, and be successful based on most traditional measures of success used in higher education. As a result, Indigenous populations are often overlooked, misunderstood, and narrowly represented in most higher education research and most institutional strategies.

Admirably filling the void of comprehensive and holistic information about Native American populations in higher education is this monograph—*Postsecondary Education for American Indians and Alaskan Natives: Higher Education for Nation Building and Self-Determination.* The authors, Bryan Brayboy, Amy Fan, Angelina Castagno, and Jessica Solyom, offer what has been missing in research and discussions about Native Americans and other Indigenous populations in higher education. They provide comprehensive information and data about Native American populations, culled from a variety of sources both traditional and nontraditional. They also provide a much needed conceptual lens—that of nation building—that helps move beyond deficit conversations to meaningful awareness of the importance of the presence and success of

Native American communities in higher education. The authors masterfully explain how this success is important to Native American students as well as their larger communities. Issues associated with sovereignty and self-determination set Native Americans apart from standard discourses about "minority" populations and diversity in higher education. The history of Native Americans in society in general, provides a unique context for understanding the educational experiences of Indigenous populations in the United States.

The monograph is brilliant in its treatment of basic background information that is useful to researchers, students, faculty, and practitioners wanting to know more about Native American populations and wanting to be more comprehensive in their research and conversations about diverse populations in higher education. The monograph pushes readers to think more critically about the context from which Native Americans come (both historically and in some instances with regard to place) and the context to which they contribute. If we just look at Native American students as another underrepresented minority that suffers from an array of problems in succeeding in traditional higher education, we fail to consider the totality of history and driving concepts like self-governance. This monograph demonstrates why it is not possible to portray the history and experiences of Native Americans in higher education accurately absent a holistic perspective.

In the ASHE monograph series as a whole we have intentionally addressed issues related to comprehensive understandings about diversity in higher education. Monographs, for example, by Marybeth Walpole on low SES students, by Rachelle Winkle-Wagner on cultural capital, and by Amy Bergeson on college choice and access, are complementary to this monograph on Indigenous students in higher education. However, this monograph really does stand alone in recognizing the unique situation and circumstances of a particular population (i.e., Native Americans) while providing a critical and theoretical lens through which to view the success of the Native American community in higher education. This is not a monograph that expresses the problems and deficits of an underrepresented minority; rather it offers a complex understanding of an important constituency that is rooted in the history and culture of Indigenous populations in the United States.

Above all else, you will find this monograph an informative, good read. It will appeal to and be helpful to multiple audiences, including college and university administrators, researchers, graduate students, and anyone interested in Native Americans in higher education. The monograph can serve as a model to many by showing the importance of looking at groups of students from a larger historical and cultural context and showing the importance of asking "what's wrong with higher education" rather than asking "what's wrong with 'them'." The concepts of sovereignty and nation building serve as important reminders for those within higher education to take into consideration not only where people come from, but also where they are going. We hope you learn from and enjoy this monograph as much as we did.

Kelly Ward and Lisa Wolf-Wendel
Series Editors

Acknowledgments

This monograph actually began to take shape in different parts of the United States simultaneously. In early 2000, Bryan was working on a piece for a journal article that offered an overview of the experiences of Indigenous undergraduate students in higher education. Six years later, he revised and expanded the overview with Angelina. Simultaneously, in the early part of the first decade of the twenty-first century, Amy was working on examining the transitions from high school to college and the role that tribal education departments played in Native students attending college. These pieces came together in this monograph; Jessica played a vital role in the past year in working on the nation-building components of this monograph. We acknowledge the early work of Bobby Wright, Michael Pavel, Arthur C. Parker, Vine Deloria, Jr., and John Tippeconnic III, and the more recent work of Heather Shotton, Lee Bitsoi, and Stephanie Waterman.

Bryan acknowledges Angelina and Jessica for working with him on this project over the last five years; they have been wonderful writing and thinking partners over the past eight years. He also wants to thank Amy for broaching the idea of a book-length manuscript as a way to bring the work together. Bryan is grateful to Bill Tierney for broaching the idea of an overview of American Indians in higher education in 2000; sadly, he was unable to finish that project, but Bill pressed for its completion. This monograph is partly his vision. Bryan's colleague, Terri McCarty, has encouraged him in innumerable ways. Bryan's friend and colleague Malia Villegas' work on nation building among the Maori in Aotearoa/New Zealand and conversations around the concept of nation building inspired and guided him. Finally, Bryan would like to thank his spouse, Doris Warriner, and their children Quanah and Ely, for putting up with him while he worked on the project, at times forsaking familial responsibilities. He hopes for Quanah and Ely—two beautiful, Indigenous boys—that their experiences in college will be better than those described in this monograph.

Amy would like to thank all those who helped to make this monograph possible. Her gratitude extends to her coauthors for their hard work and insights on this project, other Native scholars whose research is referenced throughout this monograph, and the Association for the Study of Higher Education (ASHE) for providing a space for conversations about American Indian/Alaska Native higher education issues and how to improve postsecondary educational opportunities and outcomes for Native students and faculty. Without the support of ASHE, this monograph may not have come to fruition. Finally, Amy would like to acknowledge her family, friends, colleagues, and students who encourage and support her in this work.

Angelina is incredibly grateful to Bryan for his leadership on this project, as well as his consistent friendship and guidance. Many of her understandings about higher education, Indigenous communities, and collaboration have been shaped by Bryan. She also wants to thank her partner and husband, Tyler, for understanding when this project crept into family camping trips, thwarted attempts to enjoy a leisurely breakfast, and otherwise occupied her energy. Although her children, Tarek and Keelan, were too young to know what it meant when mom had to work, they provided inspiration for her to stay focused and work efficiently. She could not have done this work without the support of her mom, who cared for her boys when she and Tyler could not. She dedicates this monograph to her mom, for her unwavering generosity.

Jessica, first and foremost, wishes to acknowledge and thank Dr. Bryan Brayboy, for mentoring her over the years, for serving as an academic and personal guide in her life, and for helping to refine her thinking on many of the ideas presented in this text, especially issues of sovereignty, self-determination, and nation building. She is additionally grateful to Angelina and Amy for inviting her on board to participate in the process of creating this monograph. Jessica is deeply grateful to the many Indigenous women and leaders whose strength and fortitude, whose voices and insight, have nurtured her thinking, guided her actions, and inspired her so much over the years. This work is dedicated to them and to the Indigenous youth whose dreams and everyday actions lead them to contribute to the peace and strength of their families and nation(s). Lastly, Jessica wishes to thank her family, especially her grandfather, for granting her the support, love, and inspiration for engaging in this work.

Published online in Wiley Online Library
(wileyonlinelibrary.com) • DOI: 10.1002/aehe.3705

Introduction

THIS MONOGRAPH SYNTHESIZES what we know about higher education among American Indian and Alaska Native[1] students. Although
progress in educational attainment has been made, compared to all other racialized student groups, Indigenous students have the highest high school drop-
out rates (Swanson, 2004), are least likely to have completed college preparatory
courses in high school (Chavers, 2002; Greene and Forster, 2003; Planty,
Bozick, and Ingels, 2006), and have among the lowest college entrance and
retention rates in the country (Devoe and Darling-Churchill, 2008; Hunt
and Harrington, 2008). After decades of national-, state-, and institutional-level
initiatives to increase access to higher education, the college pipeline for American
Indian and Alaska Native students remains largely unaddressed. As a result, little is known and even less is understood about the critical issues, conditions, and
postsecondary transitions of this incredibly diverse group of students.

As we walk the reader through what we do know about higher education
for Indigenous students, we weave central themes of tribal nation building,
sovereignty, self-determination, Indigenous knowledge systems, and culturally
responsive schooling throughout the discussion (see, for example, Barnhardt
and Kawagley, 2005; Battiste, 2002; Brayboy, 2005a; Brayboy and Maughan,
2009; Castagno and Brayboy, 2008; Deloria and Wildcat, 2001; Lomawaima
and McCarty, 2006). As Austin (2005) notes, if institutions of higher education were more knowledgeable about the unique political status of Indigenous
people and nations, they would better understand students and the institution's responsibility toward Indigenous students and communities. We take this
guidance seriously and attempt not only to shed light on what the current body

of research literature tells us about postsecondary education, but also to encourage a deeper understanding of issues central and unique to Indigenous students and tribal nations.

There are a number of ways in which Indigenous students and communities remain absent from the fabric of mainstream institutions of higher education. The notions of competition and individual success are often at odds with the reasons many Indigenous students pursue postsecondary education in the first place—to serve their families and communities better (Brayboy, 2005b). Serving families and communities is one part of the larger concept of nation building, which is a fundamental part of our project. We draw on the work of Indigenous scholars and delve into the international literature on the topic, and we will enter into a significant overview of what we mean by nation building and its implications for American Indians in institutions of higher education in the chapter entitled "Framing the Conversation."

Making communities healthy through the pursuit of self-determination and tribal sovereignty is rarely acknowledged within the paradigms that guide higher-education discussions about recruitment, retention, and success. The often-used postsecondary metaphor of the "educational pipeline" is just one example of the ways in which higher education (inadvertently) marginalizes Indigenous people and communities. We know that many Indigenous students who pursue postsecondary education often do so over a number of years, with breaks for various reasons, and by attending multiple institutions before completing a single degree. As long as success along the pipeline continues to be defined as completing a degree within four to six years of consistent, full-time enrollment at a single institution, Indigenous students will continue to be framed as failures in higher education.

We cannot, however, ignore statistics and reports that continue to inform us that Indigenous students are not well served by mainstream institutions of higher education (for example, low matriculation and graduation rates, feelings of not belonging, and encounters with racism). We suggest that institutions of higher education need to do a much better job of recruiting and retaining Indigenous students at both the undergraduate and graduate levels. Success along these paths is critical for the health of tribal nations, the pursuit and enactment of tribal sovereignty, and the realization of educational equity within the United States. At the same time, institutions of higher education must also acknowledge that Indigenous students and communities may not always be interested in pursuing or framing success in the same ways or for the same reasons as other students and communities. Institutions of higher education, leaders within colleges and universities, policy makers, and faculty and staff must be able to hold these two points in constant, and creative, tension if the goal is to serve Indigenous students and communities better.

Situating American Indian and Alaska Native Higher Education in Larger Contexts

Institutions of higher education do not operate in vacuums free of context and all that surround them; they are intimately tied to the larger contexts of communities, states, and nations. Understanding American Indian and Alaska Native participation in postsecondary education, then, requires some knowledge of Indigenous communities and tribal nations broadly speaking.

It is important to address some basic issues initially as we move forward throughout the text. Throughout this text, we use American Indian, Alaska Native, Native, and Indigenous interchangeably. We understand that there are differences in how these terms are used and understood, and want to outline our views regarding the use of these terms briefly. Naming, of course, is always political; we recognize this, although our hope in the process is to not engage in identity politics of who is or is not a "real" Native person. That is both beyond the scope of our project and beyond the scope of who we are. Native nations define their members. We fully understand that American Indians and Alaska Natives are engaged differently by the federal courts and, in some instances, by other branches. Indeed, among Native peoples in the continental United States (or the lower forty-eight states), there are differences between federally and state recognized tribes. When the Alaska Native Claims Settlement Act (ANCSA) was signed in 1971 by Richard Nixon, Alaska Native peoples' land claims were effectively extinguished so that oil being drilled in the northern part of the state could be carried through a pipeline to the southern part of the state for transport to refineries in the continental United States. To this end, the relationship between the federal government and the Alaska

Native peoples is somewhat different because of legal relationships regarding land. But the U.S. Department of Education does have programs recognizing the unique status of Alaska Native peoples and the unique relationships between the U.S. government and Alaska Native peoples.

American Indian peoples, or those who inhabit the continental United States, signed over 350 treaties with the United States and in the process ceded one billion acres of land (for example, see Deyhle and Swisher, 1997). In the process, these treaties and resulting legislation, both implicitly and explicitly, promised American Indian peoples access to health care and educational services, and provided for their general welfare (Deloria and Lytle, 1983). Relations between the federal government and tribal nations, however, grew complicated when, in 1953, House Concurrent Resolution 108 was passed. The passage of HCR 108 eventually led to the termination of the government-to-government relationships between the United States and 109 tribal nations (for example, see Deloria and Lytle, 1983, and Wilkins, 2002). This was complicated even further by Public Law 280, which gave state governments civil and criminal jurisdiction over reservations, in large part to relieve federal financial obligations to tribes (Goldberg-Ambrose, 1997).

For the purposes of this monograph, we do not delve into the major differences between state- versus federally-recognized tribes. There is much contention around this topic, because of the ways that federal recognition has been taken up to signify that a group is real only if it is recognized by the federal government. Our take is that American Indian peoples that have forms of government and have, over time, invoked their rights as Indigenous peoples fall within our discussion in this text. That is, we believe that sovereignty and nationhood are, as Deloria and Lytle (1983) note, extraconstitutional. They precede the Constitution and are not dependent upon it or on recognition from the U.S. government. American Indians then, for us, constitute peoples that claim their status as Indigenous peoples in relation to either the federal or state government.

The term *Indigenous* indicates a group of people who have been tied to a particular place before any outside peoples were introduced to the lands. We intentionally capitalize Indigenous to indicate that this references peoples with inherent rights because of their status as original peoples. In some cases, the term *Indigenous* has been used as a way to indicate solidarity between Native peoples across the globe with special ties to place and an engagement with colonialism.

In the 1970s, the use of the term *Native* came into popular usage to connote that American Indians were native to the land that is the United States. Many people who are American Indian still refer to themselves as Native American or simply Native. Many of the laws governing Indigenous issues in the United States refer specially to American Indians (and Alaska Natives), although there are some that refer to Native Americans. We choose to use both terms, interchangeably, to capture the totality of how people refer to themselves. We want to be clear, however, that we reject the claims of people who call themselves Native American because they were born in the United States. These people may be native to the United States, but we are not referencing them when we discuss Native Americans; we are referring to individuals who have ancestry tied to Indigenous peoples.

There is a range and diversity in both the day-to-day experiences and the history of tribal peoples across the United States. Indigenous peoples from tribes on the east coast came into contact with Europeans well before many in the plains and southwest areas. Across the country, there are Indigenous groups who speak their Native languages daily, but many more who do not; those who are involved in subsistence activities and others who are not. In short, some Native peoples engage in hunting and gathering on their traditional lands in the ways that are reminiscent of the ways that their ancestors engaged in subsistence; others engage in hunting and gathering at Safeway, Albertsons, and Trader Joe's. Still other Native peoples dance powwow, whereas others have never been to a powwow. These diverse experiences are expected and illustrative.

We discuss the commonalities of experiences of Native students and faculty in this monograph; we do so, however, with an understanding that there is a range and variation in these experiences. We believe that the commonalities are important in addressing the role of higher education in the lives of Native peoples across the United States. One final note before we outline a brief history of Indigenous peoples in the United States—we have not included Native Hawaiians in this study. Not doing so is rooted in a few reasons. First, the data on Native Hawaiians are complicated in how they are reported; these data are often included with Asian/Pacific Islanders. Second, the data that exist are slight. Finally, it seems to us that attempting to address these data are beyond our scope of expertise. It is clear, from our vantage point, that Native Hawaiians share much in common with other Indigenous peoples and that future work must find ways to address their experiences. An examination of the experiences of Native Hawaiians is an area not only worthy of study, but one that is desperately needed as well. Having argued for its need, we recognize that we do not—nor did we intend to—address this important issue. We hope someone will do so in the future.

Most higher education professionals appear to be unaware of the unique histories—which have present-day realities attached to them—of Indigenous peoples in the United States. American Indians have inhabited the lands on what is now called the United States well before it was the United States. There are treaty rights that promise educational resources and benefits; some acknowledgement of this is evident in the 2004 Executive Order 13336. The Executive Order in Section 1 notes, "The United States has a unique legal relationship with Indian tribes and a special relationship with Alaska Native entities as provided in the Constitution of the United States, treaties, and Federal statutes." It goes on to document the ways that these rights are engaged through educational programs. It is important to note that this recognition of tribal nations as political entities is vital to the suggestions we make throughout our text. These resources and the benefits of higher education are also visible in other documents and understandings around treaties and trust responsibility. Because of their unique status and history in the United States, Indigenous peoples likely engage in higher education differently as well. Tribal peoples have, in many ways, redefined the role of higher education; this redefinition is tied to ideas and concepts that we will address in this text, like Indigenous knowledge systems, sovereignty, self-determination, and nation building.

Historical Background of American Indian and Alaska Native Higher Education

For the European colonists, the lure of America was, in part, its reportedly wide-open, uninhabited land. The presence of Indigenous people on the

American continents held little significance for the colonists, because they viewed the Native people simply as savage, heathen, and uncivilized. By constructing American Indians in this way, the stage was set for White colonists to colonize the eastern seaboard rapidly and later expand further West, pushing many Indigenous peoples westward as well. As part of their colonizing efforts, the colonists attempted to educate a select group of American Indians, who would then serve as cultural conduits by returning to their communities in order to help show the light to others and pull them along to a more enlightened way of living (D. W. Adams, 1998; Almeida, 1997; Crum, 1989; Duchene, 1988; Havighurst, 1981; Oppelt, 1990; Szasz, 1999; Wright, 1988, 1990a, 1990b; Wright and Tierney, 1991). Ironically, the founders of these educational programs forgot that these so-called infidels and their ancestors assisted the enlightened in initially surviving harsh and unforgiving winters, nature, and limited food supplies and contributed much to the eventual development of the American political system.

In Henrico, Virginia, the English set aside one thousand acres for the construction of a "college for Children of the Infidels" in 1617 (Wright and Tierney, 1991). The Indigenous peoples in this area responded to such cultural intrusions with resistance. The wars between the Powhatan and the British in 1622, although not ultimately successful in expelling the colonists from the Virginian Natives' territory, *were* successful in ending the colonists' initial schemes for the construction of an American Indian college. But Indigenous resistance did not permanently halt the colonists' efforts. Harvard University was established in 1636, and in 1654 university officials built an Indian College with room to house thirty American Indian students. Records indicate, however, that only a few Native students actually stayed at the college, and those that did generally suffered from diseases (Oppelt, 1990). The charters of both William and Mary College in 1693 and Dartmouth College in 1769 reaffirmed the English desire to educate tribal nations. William and Mary built a house for Native students, and Dartmouth was founded primarily for the education of American Indians. Like Harvard, however, neither William and Mary nor Dartmouth actually matriculated many Indigenous students. By 1932, only 385 American Indians had been enrolled in postsecondary institutions and only 52 had actually graduated. The fact that only fifty-two Native students received postsecondary degrees in the United States in almost three hundred years attests to the cultural, emotional, and integration struggles these students faced and the inappropriateness of the White education system available to them during this time period. But, in some ways, times are changing; in other ways, the experiences of present-day Indigenous students are not far removed from those of the past. One point of this monograph is to examine what it means to be an Indigenous student in an institution of higher education in the twenty-first century.

A significant lack of funding for Indigenous students also contributed to their historically low attendance numbers, and when more scholarships were offered in the 1930s, the number of matriculating American Indian students increased dramatically. Whereas in 1932 only five postsecondary schools offered American Indian scholarships, the New Deal era of 1930s, the post–World War II GI bill, and the Bureau of Indian Affairs (BIA) higher education scholarship grant program resulted in two thousand enrolled Native students in the late 1950s and seven thousand by 1965. Similarly, although sixty-six American Indian graduates could be counted nationwide in 1961, by 1968 that number had tripled. Even with these drastically improved numbers, still only 1 percent of the Indigenous population of the United States in the late 1960s was enrolled in any institution of higher education (National Center for Education Statistics [NCES], 2005a). Although these higher numbers of Indigenous college students might be indicative of the expansion of the dominant notion of who is deserving of a higher education in the United States, little had changed with regard to the assimilationist aspect of mainstream, White-dominated American education. Although more Indigenous students were attending mainstream colleges and universities, they were still expected to leave their tribal cultures at home, because schools, after all, were designed to "kill the Indian and save the man."[2] These programs all failed in their quest for educating Indigenous people in the United States. Many of the original participants died; others simply left to return home for a way of life that was familiar.

Fortunately, by the 1960s new opportunities for Indigenous students were being developed. Norman Oppelt captures the general sentiment of the times when he states that, "the basic premise of white education—all persons were to be assimilated into white middle class values and behaviors—was antithetical to tribal desires to preserve some of their culture. This long-standing conflict of educational objectives was the primary impetus for the significant changes in Indian higher education that took place in the 1960s and 1970s (Oppelt, 1990). Although federal money had been supporting American Indian Studies programs at mainstream institutions and scholarships for Indigenous students at these institutions since the 1950s, tribal leaders began arguing that federal money spent on programs and students at mainstream schools could be better spent by directly supporting tribal communities. The brain drain from reservations was depleting human resources and causing many young American Indians to leave their tribal homes. This desire to keep American Indians in their own communities, combined with the relative economic prosperity many tribes experienced in the 1960s and the national community college movement occurring at that time, led to the rapid development of a number of tribal colleges.

Now, more than three centuries since the establishment of White-controlled colleges for the education of Indigenous people, and three decades since the first tribal colleges were established, Indigenous students still make up only 1 percent of the total enrollment in institutions of higher education. This monograph attempts to contextualize the state of higher education for Indigenous people in the United States. Although American Indians and Alaska Natives appear to be the most researched group of racialized students in K–12 education (Deyhle and Swisher, 1997), they are arguably the least-studied group in higher education. Very little research has been conducted that specifically examines Indigenous people in higher education and in college, and even less has been conducted on success within institutions of higher education.

Overview of the Monograph

This monograph reviews and synthesizes what we know regarding Indigenous undergraduate and graduate students and faculty in higher education. We believe it is important to differentiate between the experiences of undergraduate students, graduate students, and faculty because it provides not only an overview of what is occurring in institutions of higher education, but also variability in levels of experience. Although there is a fair amount of research-, theory-, and practice-based literature on this topic, it has not been brought together in a single user-friendly volume. In addition to discussing what we know, we also consider what we do not know and suggest that future analyses of Indigenous students in higher education be guided by a few central themes, including tribal nation building, Indigenous knowledge systems, and culturally responsive schooling. This monograph is guided by the following questions.

What do we know about Indigenous students' access to postsecondary education?

What do we know about Indigenous students and faculty in institutions of higher education? What do we not yet know, and how might we begin to learn some of that?

What is unique about the experiences of Indigenous students and faculty in higher education?

How and in what ways does nation building figure into an analysis of the experiences of students and faculty in institutions of higher education?

The next chapter, "Framing the Coversation" offers an overview of key concepts and an extended discussion of nation building, sovereignty, self-determination, and Indigenous knowledge systems. A chapter entitled "Postsecondary Access for Indigenous Students" focuses on issues of access to higher education. This is followed by "American Indian and Alaska Native College Students," which specifically looks at the undergraduate experience for Indigenous students. The following two chapters discuss the postbaccalaureate experiences of Indigenous graduate students and faculty within postsecondary institutions. A final chapter attempts to initiate conversations about the policy, practice, and research implications of what we know—and what we have yet to learn—about higher education for Indigenous students and communities in the United States. We suggest throughout this monograph that higher education for American Indians and Alaska Natives must be understood within the context of tribal nation building, sovereignty, and self-determination; Indigenous knowledge systems; and culturally responsive schooling.

Framing the Conversation

A SIMPLE REVIEW OF THE LITERATURE on postsecondary schooling among Indigenous peoples is not what we are attempting here. Instead, we want to suggest that conversation, research, policy, and practice regarding American Indians in higher education be framed within the context of tribal nation building.

American Indian/Alaska Native postsecondary access and persistence cannot be understood independently from the unique political status of tribes. The dual position of American Indians and Alaska Natives as both racial/ethnic groups and legal/political groups and individuals, as well as an understanding of the hundreds of years of abusive relationships between mainstream educational institutions and Native communities, are important to framing any conversation between Native peoples as both racialized and political (Brayboy, 2005a, 2005b; Shield, 2004). The American Indian/Alaska Native (AI/AN) population is the most diverse in the country, representing more than 560 distinct federally recognized tribes and at least half as many distinct state-recognized tribal groups (U.S. Department of the Interior, 2007). Each tribe has its own history, culture, and language—defying easy generalization. There is no singular "Native American experience" (Deloria, 1988). Federally recognized tribes have in common their distinctive government-to-government relationship with the federal government, and their enrolled members have the benefit of *dual citizenship* wherein they do not lose civil rights because of their status as tribal citizens and individual tribal citizens are not denied tribal rights because of their American citizenship (Deloria and Lytle, 1983, as cited in Grande, 2004). American Indians have not, like other marginalized groups, been fighting for inclusion into the democratic body politic; rather, they have, and continue to, assert their right to remain distinct, sovereign, and tribal peoples (Alfred, 1999, 2005; Cornell and Kalt, 1998; Grande, 2004; D.E. Wilkins, 2002). One way to understand this fight is in the context of tribal nation building, and it is, from our perspectives, central to conversations about higher education among Indigenous peoples.

Tribal Nation Building

The international research literature has often conceptualized nation building as a liberal democratic project that frames aspects of belonging (citizenship), national identity, language, and rights within in a larger global context (Dhamoon and Abu-Laban, 2009; Etzioni, 2009/2010). Many of these projects may be based on a colonial approach that focuses on the imposition of a common culture and the gradual homogenization of values within a society, often with a bias toward the particular experience of European societies against non-Western values (Alfred, 1995, p. 8). However, for Indigenous communities in the United States, the term *nation* usually implies a specific combination of kinship, government, shared territory, worldview, and spiritual community (Champagne, 2008). Drawing from the work of Akoto (1992), we understand nation building as "the conscious and focused application of [Indigenous] people's collective resources, energies, and knowledge to the task of liberating and developing the psychic and physical space that is identified as [their] own" (p. 3). The process of nation building consists of many layers, including the development of behaviors, values, language, institutions, and physical structures that elucidate the community's history and culture, infuse and protect knowledge of the past in present-day practices, and ensure the future identity and independence of the nation (Akoto, 1992).

Additionally, Alfred (2005), when discussing the concept of *wasáse*, presents us with a particular type of Indigenous nation-building project that is both an ethical and political project centered not on an anticolonization approach, but a process of decolonization. Alfred's approach emphasizes the strengthening of political, economic, social, cultural, and spiritual processes within Indigenous communities. Other scholars have offered definitions of nation building that include goals such as strengthening identity, building social capital, defending sovereignty, exercising sovereignty, and providing for the nation's well-being (Cornell and Kalt, 1998, 2006, 2010; Jorgenson, 2007). These goals can be accomplished by focusing on aspects of political self-rule, including placing an emphasis on building legal, political, and juridical practices based on community belief systems and practices (Cornell and Kalt, 1998, 2006, 2010; Helton, 2003/2004; Jorgenson, 2007); localized managing of health and healing practices, services, and the institutions that offer these services (Cornell and Kalt, 2010); economic development (Blain, 2010; Cornell and Kalt, 1998, 2006, 2010; Jorgenson, 2007); and educational development (Alfred, 1999, 2005; Champagne, 2004; St. Germaine, 2008; Lynch, 2004). Ultimately, for us, the process of nation building consists of legal and political, cultural, economic, health and nutrition, spiritual, and educational elements with the well-being, sovereignty, self-determination, and autonomy of the community as the driving force for nation building.

The extant literature suggests there are two prevailing models for nation building in Indigenous communities. The first model frames nation building primarily through an economic-development lens (Cornell and Kalt, 1992; Frickey, 1997; Helton, 2003/2004; Pommersheim, 1984). This model integrates a consideration of the juridical, legal, and political aspects that reflect the community's values and culture and is ultimately intended to enable the Indigenous community to become autonomous and independent from the economic control of outside sources (including the federal government). The second model of nation building incorporates an emphasis on economic development but does not centralize it. Rather, the second view of nation building includes an emphasis on legal/political, cultural, economic, health/nutrition, and education aspects. Both models place sovereignty, self-determination, and autonomy of the community as the driving force for nation building. In this text, we ascribe to this latter model of nation building. We do not reject the economic focus of others' components of nation building; instead, our intent here is to extend, complicate, and nuance what Cornell, Kalt, and others have advanced as it relates to American Indians in higher education.

For us, nation building as a political, ethical, and cultural project is deliberate, "keenly directed and focused" (Akoto, 1992), and directly linked to sovereignty and self-determination. We will offer a more complete understanding of sovereignty later in the chapter, but for now we turn our attention to the notion of self-determination. Cornell and Kalt (2010) explain the importance of self-determination for Indigenous communities with the passage in 1975 of the Indian Self-Determination and Education Assistance Act (U.S. Public Law 95-638). This act, which ushered in a number of formal policies of tribal self-determination, set the wheels in motion for Indigenous communities to begin to (re)claim the vision and driving forces behind their economic, political, legal, and educational processes. Indigenous community members sought to engage the discourse, policy, and structures of their community actively, in hopes of better addressing the particular and unique needs of their community. Early attempts at self-rule were laborious, confusing, and challenging at times, because many Indigenous nations had historically utilized governmental systems modeled on foreign and colonial (that is, non-Indigenous) values, structures, and processes. Many nations also lacked meaningful experience in business and governmental decision making among the living population, and bore legacies of oppressive and violent federally imposed systems of education. By the second half of the 1980s, however, self-determination had become more focused and widespread. Systematic restructuring of tribal governments and their relations with the federal government ensued (Cornell and Kalt, 2010). This restructuring began to be known as the nation-building movement and is now currently being manifested by wholesale changes in tribal institutions and policies as Indigenous nations, themselves, rewrite their constitutions, generate increasing shares of revenues through their own taxes and business enterprises, establish their own courts and law-enforcement systems, remake school curricula, and so on (Cornell and Kalt, 2010).

The U.S. federal government's policy of self-determination through self-governance by American Indian nations has evolved and changed over the last forty years. Yet, at its core it has been consistently predicated on two principles: providing greater control to tribal citizens and their governments in planning, designing, implementing, and controlling the public affairs of their respective tribes; and maintaining the trust relationship between the federal government and American Indian tribes (Cornell and Kalt, 2010). The policy of self-determination entails explicit federal promotion of government-to-government relations between tribes and the U.S. government. This is intended to minimize the historically pervasive presence of the federal government in tribal government, provide services to Native Americans, and select and implement economic and community development plans and projects in tribal communities (Cornell and Kalt, 2010). We agree, however, with Alfred (1999) and Helton (2003/2004) that Indigenous nations cannot successfully engage in nation-building projects that are driven by sovereignty and self-determination unless they develop independence of mind by taking action to restore pride in their traditions, languages, and knowledge. The arduous process of reasserting sovereignty begins not solely with the nation's land or (re)claiming economic and political processes (though we recognize that this is important!), but with sovereignty of the peoples' minds (Coffey and Tsosie, 2001; Helton, 2003/2004).

Indigenous Knowledge Systems

We believe that the project of developing an independence of mind in order to develop a vision for nation building must be based in (re)claiming Indigenous knowledge systems. We recognize that there lies great diversity among Indigenous peoples: hundreds of languages, a broad range of customs in the social and political realms, and a complex variety of spiritual beliefs. Yet we believe Indigenous peoples share a common bond. This common bond rests on a commitment to a profoundly respectful way of governing based on worldview that balances respect for autonomy with recognition of a universal interdependency and promotes peaceful coexistence among all elements of creation (Alfred, 1999; Akoto, 1992). Indigenous knowledges have the capacity to break down presumed barriers between reservation and urban, full-blood and mixed blood, and makes it difficult to question the lived experiences of Indigenous individuals and communities. These knowledges form a coherent sense of how to view the world that is driven by principles that transcend the cultural, linguistic, and social and political differences across Indigenous communities and members. Moreover, the passing on and acquisition of these knowledges inform the everyday existence of Indigenous peoples. Battiste (2002, p. 7) explains, "Indigenous knowledge is systemic, covering both what can be observed and what can be thought. It comprises the rural and the urban, the settled and the nomadic, original inhabitants and migrants." Ultimately, Indigenous knowledges and ways of arriving at such knowledge are context specific and rooted in the lived experiences of individuals and communities.

At the heart of Indigenous knowledge systems are notions of community and its concomitant survival; an understanding that lived experience is a very important form of knowledge (and subsequently informs theory); the importance of relationality, respect, and reciprocity; as well as recognition of the importance of place/space and land. In this paradigm, the survival of Indigenous community is more important than any individual. This is because individuals, through the continual process of self-discovery and selflessness, become whole; thereby ensuring community survival. Lomawaima and McCarty (2006) write, "The ultimate test of each human educational system is a people's survival" (p. 30). This sentiment is captured through Burkhart's (2004) insightful reworking of the Cartesian principle. Descartes' work, which centered on the individual and rational thought processes, grounded his philosophies of knowing and ontologies through the principle that says, "I think, therefore I am." Yet Burkhart argues that an Indigenous version of this principle is "We are, therefore I am." At its core, then, the knowledge systems, ways of being, and teaching philosophies for many Indigenous peoples are critically focused on community and survival. In contrast, far from feeling a sense of responsibility to others, the Western individualist philosophy inherent in the colonialist consciousness is manifested in the genocide of Indigenous peoples, their dispossession, their marginalization, and extreme damage to the ecosystem. When relationships are seen as pervasive and profound, they require attention. Proper attention to relationships requires effort toward their maintenance, and it requires reciprocity.

A reciprocal relationship exists where communities act to support individuals and individuals act with the best interests of their communities in mind. What do we mean by reciprocity? Reciprocity, as we mean it here, is not simply a quid pro quo or a sense of "you scratch my back and I'll scratch yours." Instead, it is a sense that individuals must act outside of their self-interests for those of the community and work toward their own betterment for the community's sake. The point here is that individual development happens for the betterment of community. Additionally, those who are given gifts of guidance, shared wisdom, and teachings must give this to others. If we consider the connections between the past, present, and future, this comes into deeper clarity.

For community members or allies, who are given gifts, their responsibility is to ensure the community's survival. One way of doing this is by responding to the needs of the youth and sharing that knowledge (and its concomitant power, where appropriate) with the next generation. Simply stated, reciprocity is guided by the mantra, "We give so that others can take, for our survival. We take so that we can give to others. Those who receive must give what they have to others." Only through reciprocity can community survival be possible. This simple fact points to one of the reasons for the centrality of the community instead of the individual. Individuals play a role in the survival of communities; they can never come before it. Thus, the purpose of knowledge, first and foremost, is to ensure personal growth, rooted in relationships with other members of the community and with the places the community inhabits. Whitt (2004) describes knowledge sharing as gift giving. As such, she contends, "It is, after all, the givers of gifts who must determine when, to whom, and how the gifts are to be given" (p. 209). Further, she argues that the recipient of a gift has a responsibility to that gift and the person or community who shared it with him/her. This gift giving relies on principles of reciprocity.

We have discussed above the importance and role of self-determination in a nation-building agenda, as well as the connections between self-determination and Indigenous knowledge systems within a framework of nation building. Now we turn to a more detailed outline of what we mean by *sovereignty*. In short, we take sovereignty to be the inherent right of tribal nations to direct their futures and engage the world in ways that are meaningful to them. Self-determination is the engagement of sovereignty; put another way, self-determination is the *operationalization* of sovereignty.

Sovereignty, Self-Determination, and Self-Governance

The sovereign status of Native American tribes, as Chief Justice John Marshall commented, is like no other in the world. We will not cover the entire history of conceptions of sovereignty for Indigenous peoples, as others (Alfred, 1999, 2005; Barker, 2005; Deloria and Lytle, 1983; Wilkins, 2001; Williams, 1997) have covered this ground remarkably well.[3] The topic of sovereignty has not been fully engaged by scholars primarily interested in education; there are, of course, notable exceptions to this (K. B. Adams, 1988; Archibald, 2001; Battiste, 2000, 2002; Battiste and Barman, 1995; Lomawaima, 2000; Lomawaima and McCarty, 2006; L. T. Smith, 1999) that we believe are quite useful to the arguments outlined in this monograph.

On April 30, 2004, President George W. Bush signed Executive Order 13336. The purpose of the executive order was to "assist American Indian and Alaska Native students in meeting the challenging student academic standards of the 'No Child Left Behind Act' in a manner that is consistent with Tribal traditions, languages, and cultures" (Federal Register, 2004). Most critically, Bush recognized the unique political and legal relationship of tribal governments:

> *The United States has a unique legal relationship with Indian tribes and a special relationship with Alaska Native entities as provided in the Constitution of the United States, treaties, and Federal statutes. This Administration is committed to continuing to work with these Federally recognized tribal governments on a government-to-government basis, and supports tribal sovereignty and self-determination. It is the purpose of this order to assist American Indian and Alaska Native students in meeting the challenging student academic standards of the No Child Left Behind Act of 2001 (Public Law 107–110) in a manner that is consistent with tribal traditions, languages, and cultures [President George W. Bush; Federal Register, 2004].*

From this proclamation, it appears the U.S. federal government recognizes the sovereignty and inherent rights of tribal nations. In present terms, sovereignty is an engagement of legal and political relationships between tribal nations in the United States and the U.S. government. Tribal nations, under this legal/political iteration of sovereignty, are distinct entities that have the right to self-govern based on their traditional and self-selected processes. Helton (2003/2004) notes, "Even as 'dependent domestic nations,' tribes retain the pre-constitutional right of self-determination and internal self-government . . . Native Nations may select their own model of governance" (p. 9).

Indian tribes are delineated by the United States as "domestic dependent nations," and the relationship between such tribes and the U.S. government "resembles that of a ward to his guardian" (*Cherokee Nation v. Georgia* and *Worcester v. Georgia*). The Constitution, following the previous centralized English model of handling Indian policy, identifies Congress (Article 1, Section 8) as the proper body empowered to regulate commerce with the Indian tribes. Concurrently, the Supreme Court has long recognized and defined the "peculiar relationship" between Indian tribes and the federal government. In fact, it is the early interpretations of the Constitution by Chief Justice John Marshall that form the basis of much of modern Indian law.

Yet, when prefaced with the word *tribal*, Native peoples, in effect, have claimed ownership of the term *sovereignty* (Wilkins, 2004). According to Wilkins (2004), *tribal* reflects the relational and horizontal aspects of Indigenous communities, and encompasses the territorial, cultural, and politi-cal nature of Native societies. As one can see, *tribal sovereignty* articulates intersecting worldviews and definitions. On the one hand, it represents an unusual relationship with the federal government, defined by early treaties and court cases in the eighteenth and nineteenth centuries. On the other hand, tribal sovereignty represents a communal process and encompasses multiple dimensions: inherent, political/legal, economic, cultural, and educational aspects where all features are inextricably linked and are defined by the particularity of individual tribes. Subsequently, contradictory, ideological, and structural interconnections between the recognition of tribal sovereignty and the notion that the U.S. Congress has virtually unlimited authority over tribal nations, their governments, their rights, and their resources continue to be at the forefront of any meaningful discussions of these issues. Alfred (1999), however, continues to illuminate the importance of Indigenous-controlled models of government when he says, "if the new governments do not embody a notion of power that is appropriate to indigenous cultures, the goals of the struggle will have been betrayed. Leaders who promote non-indigenous goals and embody non-indigenous values are simply tools used by the state to maintain its control. The spiritual connections and fundamental respect for each other and for the earth that were our ancestors' way and the foundations of our traditional systems must be restored" (p. xiv).

Clearly, Executive Order 13336 points to the political and legal aspects of sovereignty. Namely, it is rooted in nation-to-nation relationships. We recognize the importance of this form of sovereignty, but agree with Coffey and Tsosie (2001), who warn, "In a world where tribal political sovereignty is dependent upon federal acknowledgement, Indian nations will always be vulnerable to restrictions of their sovereignty and perhaps even to the total annihilation of their sovereignty" (p. 194). Although we believe that the legal and political aspects of sovereignty are important, we also believe that there is significant merit in the Coffey and Tsosie (2001) conception of "cultural sovereignty."

Coffey and Tsosie (2001, p. 191) write, "cultural sovereignty is a process of reclaiming culture and of building nations." They note that conversations regarding cultural sovereignty must account for three important inquiries. First is a question of where to "'locate' cultural sovereignty within their existing social structures and order" (p. 196). Ultimately, they note that the place for the question of location is in relationships between people and the places they live. Second, is addressing "the relationship between Native peoples' political and cultural sovereignty" (p. 196). In response, they draw a juxtaposition between legal remedies and treatments of sovereignty with cultural aspects that include spiritual components. That is, there is a philosophical view that humans and the communities of which they are a part must consider their spiritual relationships with land and ceremony. Coffey and Tsosie dissect the problems of relying on the "myth of 'cultural inferiority' to justify the government's authority to forcibly assimilate and acculturate Indian people for their own good" (p. 201) to call upon a reinvisioning of a reality of the educational, scientific, economic, and cultural resources that tribal communities have been drawing on for their continued survival over millenia.

Third, Coffey and Tsosie (2001) note that an inquiry must be made that, "probe[s] the philosophical core of our belief systems as Native peoples and creates our own appraisal of what 'sovereignty' means, what 'autonomy' means, and what rights, duties, and responsibilities are entailed in our relationships" (p. 196). Regarding this final inquiry, they contend that Indigenous peoples must engage in the process of "repatriation" (p. 202). Of this, they write, "the process of reclaiming history, tradition, and cultural identity is a process of repatriation" (p. 202). Those things to be repatriated include "wisdom" (p. 203) often included and embedded within "stories" (p. 203), "cultural identity" (p. 206), and "spirituality" (p. 208). In the wisdom of Indigenous people's relationships with place and one another, their return to a sense of tradition with an awareness of the present, and an understanding that there is an internal sense of peoplehood, "cultural sovereignty is an *internal* phenomenon: the 'heart and soul' of the Indian nation is located *within* Indian people, as communities and individuals" (p. 203, emphasis in the original).

In the end, Coffey and Tsosie (2001, p. 210) argue, "The concept of cultural sovereignty encompasses the spiritual, emotional, mental, and physical aspects of our lives. Because of this, only Native peoples can decide what the ultimate contours of Native sovereignty will be." Nation building, as a concept, relies, at least in part, on cultural sovereignty. Individuals who sacrifice and commit to earning degrees from institutions of higher education, on behalf of others who are part of their community, engage in the process of exercising cultural sovereignty. There are other forms of sovereignty embedded within our conception of nation building, however.

Lyons (2000, p. 452) outlines a vision for "rhetorical sovereignty" in response to what he calls "rhetorical imperialism: the ability of dominant powers to assert control of others by setting the terms of the debate." Lyons is clear about what this means when he writes, "The people want sovereignty, and in the colonized scene of writing, rhetorical sovereignty. *As the inherent right and ability of peoples to determine their own communicative needs and desires in the pursuit of self-determination*, rhetorical sovereignty requires above all the presence of an Indian voice, speaking or writing in an ongoing context of colonization and setting at least some of the terms of debate" (p. 462, emphasis added). We agree that "setting the terms of the debate" is an integral part of nation building. Indigenous peoples often seek degrees from institutions of higher education with the hopes of altering or changing the terms of engagement and debate.

Finally, formal education can serve as a form of developing self-sufficiency that can extend to all areas of life, including knowledge of health and foodways. We believe it is worthwhile to consider seriously what Blain (2010) calls "food sovereignty" (p. ii). Drawing on the work of Glipo and Pascual (2005), Blain notes that the most commonly held definition of food sovereignty is:

. . . the Right of peoples, communities, and countries to define their own agricultural, labour, fishing, food and land policies, which are ecologically, socially, economically and culturally appropriate to their unique circumstances. It includes the true right to food and to produce food, which means that all people have the right to safe, nutritious and culturally appropriate food and to food producing resources and the ability to sustain themselves and their societies [Glipo and Pascual, 2005, p. 1, as cited in Blain, 2010, p. 32].

Blain asserts that tribal nations must work to delink from dominant food-ways in order to provide opportunities for improvement in community and individual health, reconnection to the land, and promotion of sovereignty and nation building. In short, he appears to be arguing for a return to subsistence ways of living that will allow Indigenous peoples an opportunity to access fresh, healthy foods, leading to changes in the ways that they engage the land and are engaged by it. There are, of course, important health, economic, and spiritual aspects of this move toward engaging this type of sovereignty.

Blain (2010, p. 18) notes, "Indigenous peoples have been largely forgotten in development conversations. Development projects have been targeted at nation-states and not focused on improving the conditions of Indigenous communities." Blain echoes Alfred (1999, p. 116), who writes, "only by building economic relationships and trade with other people can we really strengthen and sustain our communities. Truly valuable development consists in the learning, the skills, the business acumen, and the empowerment that flow from taking control over our lands and using them for the collective benefit in ways that are consistent with indigenous values." Further elaborating on the concept of food sovereignty, he writes, "Sustainable economic development grounded in tradition and customary law, and rooted in respect for the land, offers a way for Indigenous communities to improve their material situation and also to promote political, cultural and economic sovereignty" (Blain, 2010, p. 26). In this way, the political, economic, and cultural can be linked through the production and consumption of healthy, sustainable foods. We would extend this argument to the ways that formal education is taken up by Indigenous peoples to sustain, promote, and enhance their nation's economic, cultural, and social well-being. There is a justice-oriented notion of nation building in Blain's work that we find compelling and important to the role of education. This monograph seeks to point to the ways that Indigenous peoples utilize higher education toward the end of strengthening, sustaining, and promoting their communities.

Economic Development

The ideas of culture, rhetoric, and food sovereignty hold important implications for nation building, as they intertwine with other important elements to frame a strong model for nation building. Cornell and Kalt (1998) argue that sovereignty, nation building, and economic development are interconnected. As the argument goes, without sovereignty and nation building, economic development is likely to remain a "frustratingly elusive dream" (p. 189). Indeed, the last quarter of the twentieth century found a growing number of tribes joining the nation-building effort as a way to address desperate economic conditions. Not all of their pursuits have been fruitful. Before we go into explicating different principles and motivations that have driven economic development, we must pause to make a note of the importance of tribal lands in these efforts.

Indigenous peoples have sustained themselves on their homelands since time immemorial, but there are emerging problems. The customary economies of these nations have largely been destroyed because of land loss, environmental destruction, and culturally genocidal laws that prohibited Indigenous communities the freedom to make a living from lands that have traditionally provided for them. The devastating effects of colonialism have resulted in the destruction of Indigenous economies and have created a set of situations that render Native peoples dependent on the United States (Blain, 2010). As long as Indigenous nations continue to rely on outside sources for funding and economic support, sovereignty will continue to be limited and constrained. For this reason, discussions of Indigenous sovereignty must move beyond the political and cultural arenas to include the economic as well.

As a result of the era of self-determination ushered in by federal legislation, many tribal governments moved economic development to the top of their policy agendas; sometimes complementing federal efforts, sometimes operating at cross-purposes. But in most cases, a single approach dominated both federal and tribal activities—the "standard" approach (Cornell and Kalt, 2006). On the one hand, the standard approach entails a process of development in which decision making is short term and nonstrategic, someone other than the Indigenous nation sets the development agenda, economic development is treated as an economic problem, Indigenous culture is seen as an obstacle to development, and elected leadership serves primarily as a distributor of resources. On the other hand, the nation-building approach, with its dual focus on asserting tribal sovereignty and building the foundational, institutional capacity to exercise sovereignty effectively, provides a positive environment for sustained economic development. This approach is defined by five primary characteristics: comprehensive assertions of sovereignty or self-rule, backing up sovereignty with effective governing institutions, matching institutions to indigenous political culture, strategic orientation, and leadership dedicated to nation building (Cornell and Kalt, 2006).

A nation-building approach recognizes that a big problem facing Indigenous communities is lack of jobs and income. Without economic revenue, infrastructures intended to support community development cannot be built. Building businesses and infrastructure without a cohesive, long-term vision for the nation (that is, without nation building in mind) results in businesses that may not thrive or that benefit a few members only, thus reproducing the unequal distribution of wealth plaguing larger mainstream communities. A nation-building agenda focused on economic wealth is not driven by a desire to reproduce material, consumer culture or uneven distributions of wealth. Economic development must not serve for the material benefit of the owners but must serve to improve the living situations for Native people, as a whole, and act as a vehicle toward economic self-determination that would validate and support cultural and political sovereignty (Blain, 2010). Alfred (2005) contends that a way to counter or avoid recreating a model of economic development that benefits a select few is to engage nation building based on tradition and customary values. He argues that Indigenous efforts to restore their autonomous power, regardless of how it is termed (for example, Aboriginal self-government; Indigenous self-determination; or Native sovereignty), are founded on an "ideology of Native nationalism and a rejection of models of government rooted in European cultural values" (Alfred, 1999, p. 2).

We agree that the manner in which economic development is pursued and the guiding principles behind it matter. We also agree with Blain (2010) and Coin (2003), that economic development in Indian country must be sustainable, culturally congruent, and, most importantly, must seek to rebuild the nations and empower and liberate the people. Economic development on tribal lands is a three-legged stool that requires a land mass in trust status, a stable tribal government, and sovereignty (Coin, 2003), but development will not endure if it is not based on the Indigenous principles that have allowed Indigenous communities to survive for millenia. For example, if the nation-building economic development project is guided by a desire to build a nation "in which both businesses and human beings can flourish" (Cornell and Kalt, 1998, p. 192), economic development must not contribute to the continued exploitation of resources—including labor and land resources.

Additionally, building culturally appropriate economic models will help to improve the overall image of tribal governance in the eyes of the general public and the citizens of the nation (Blain, 2010, p. 23). This can be accomplished by developing tribal-specific and/or tribally controlled economic enterprises. These enterprises ultimately help to drive down unemployment rates and may offer job stability to community members. "There is a common thread for tribes who have been successful in this [nation building] project— their success is based not only on being able to bring people out of generations of poverty but to preserve tribal customs and the Indian way of life" (Coin, 2003, p. 6).

In agreeing with Coin (2003), Blain (2010) succinctly states "although gaming offers a ready supply of easy capital, it does not offer a long-term economic investment strategy" (p. 24). Instead, models that are built with the intention to recenter tribal control on important industries as well as to ensure enduring job opportunities for community members offer long-term success. For example, the Hupa model of economic development has included developing departments of government, including a tribal court, health and emergency services, housing and child development. Additionally, the tribe manages natural resources that were once in the hands of the Bureau of Indian Affairs, including forestry, fisheries, and wildlife, and its (ecofriendly) timber operation serves as a model for the nation. Other tribal enterprises include an aggregate and redi-mix business, a gas station, a hotel, a newspaper, and California's only licensed tribal radio station (Coin, 2003). One tribal representative explained the vision behind the model as purposeful and with long-term investment in the success and survival of its people. The model is created to employ its community members at a range of academic and employment levels. "There is opportunity here. Hupa people can come back to the reservation and practice law and medicine. They can become lawyers or teachers or auditors . . . You have to develop the laws, then it has to be institutionalized" (Coin, 2003, p. 6).

Finally, successful economic models are based on principles that encourage people to invest in the community. The desire to invest may be diverse and motivated by different factors but ultimately must serve to reduce dependence on outside sources and bolster tribal sovereignty. A nation-building model is built with the intention to inspire its members to consider a job within the community. In this way, communities can avoid "brain drain" or losing their talented and specially skilled members. Opportunities for employment must be diverse and include opportunities within and among several areas such as tribal government, a tribal enterprise, a locally owned business, or in community schools. As Cornell and Kalt (1998, p. 193) put it, investment is not just a financial matter. An investor is anybody with time or energy or ideas or skills or good will *or* dollars who is willing to bet those assets on the tribal future.

Just as the population and land mass of each tribal community varies, so too do the economic development models used. As might be predicted, what works for one community might not work for another. However, the principles that aid in sustaining the nation-building goal of economic development seem to be shared. These models are culturally appropriate and are driven by a desire to benefit the community as a whole, protect and benefit the land, and value people over profit. They are also diverse and are centered on long-term benefit over short-term profit; are driven by the overall principle of sovereignty and self-determination, and foster an environment that can allow the community ultimately to become autonomous, if not subsistent. Nation building that includes and infuses an economic-development agenda integrates Indigenous values and leadership strength to develop actions intended to benefit present and future generations. However, these models remain incomplete if they do not also include an education and healing component. It is to these areas that we now turn.

Higher Education Toward Nation Building

We want to suggest that pursuing higher education folds into a larger agenda of tribal nation building, and vice versa—that nation building cannot be fully or adequately pursued without some agenda of higher education. We do not mean to imply that Indigenous students and communities necessarily must engage mainstream, predominantly White institutions of higher education (indeed, as we discuss in later chapters, tribal colleges and universities have played important roles in the development and sustainability of healthy tribal communities). Rather, we believe that educational success within Indigenous communities is a necessary (though not sufficient) element of successful nation building.

We build upon the "cultural match" notion of The Harvard Project on American Indian Economic Development (HPAIED; 2008) and argue that the educational goals—with a particular emphasis on higher education—of Indigenous peoples, in order to be effective, must coincide with the strategic political and economic objectives and opportunities of their communities. Cornell and Kalt (2006) contend that in order for a tribe to be economically successful, it must first be politically successful. We carry that argument further, believing that in a modern-day society, and accounting for globalization and economic notions of nation building, in order for a tribe to be economically and politically successful, it must also be educationally successful.

We want to suggest further that educational success, and hence nation building, is more likely to be realized when schools seriously consider culturally responsive approaches to education. Culturally responsive schooling is a widely recognized educational approach for better serving Indigenous students in elementary and secondary schools (Castagno and Brayboy, 2008). Coming largely out of the cultural-difference literature, culturally responsive schooling assumes that a "firm grounding in the heritage language and culture indigenous to a particular tribe is a fundamental prerequisite for the development of culturally-healthy students and communities associated with that place, and thus is an essential ingredient for identifying the appropriate qualities and practices associated with culturally-responsive educators, curriculum, and schools" (Alaska Native Knowledge Network, 1998, p. 2). This educational approach requires a shift in teaching methods, curricular materials, teacher dispositions, and school–community relations. Although culturally responsive schooling is not as common in the literature on postsecondary education, we want to suggest that higher education toward nation building would require colleges and universities (and those who lead them) to provide culturally responsive schooling as well. This would entail deeper understanding of the concepts previously outlined (nation building, self-determination, Indigenous knowledge systems, and sovereignty) so that postsecondary institutions are better able to ensure broad access, healthy experiences, and successful completion to Indigenous students who can then serve their communities.

In order to construct more enduring governments and viable economic institutions, education in Indigenous communities should uphold the values, interests, and cultures of the communities and nations. In this way, new understandings of Indigenous nationhood can be conceptualized and will preserve community, sovereignty, and cultural traditions. Champagne (2004) asserts that Native students are interested and engaged in issues concerning the Native community but, unfortunately, they know little about Native rights, policy, or the status of Native communities in the United States. Additionally, students often have inaccurate or incomplete information about issues they currently face, including issues of repatriation, mascot issues, or issues addressing student admissions and recruitment to the university. This is because, for many Native students, they have never been taught the history of Native policies or issues. Thus, in order to develop a strong nation-building agenda, Indigenous nations should focus on their youth and education. Furthermore, education must be relevant to the current struggles facing youth and must aid in learning about policies, rights, and status of Indigenous peoples (and their nation) so they can aid in nation building (Champagne, 2004; St. Germaine, 2008). For Champagne, this approach toward preparing and educating youth to participate in nation-building efforts needs to be driven by Native leaders, scholars, and elders to guide and teach youth.

Additionally, Champagne (2004) recognizes the interconnectedness between sovereignty, self-determination, economic development, and education involved in nation building. For although Indigenous students may be interested in going to college to gain skills and knowledge in areas that may benefit their nation, ultimately, these skills are of little use to them if they lack firsthand knowledge or understanding of Native institutions, communities, and values. In short, the skills obtained at the university may be irrelevant to the nation. Thus graduates may have a hard time finding work and/or applying the skill set they have gained. Champagne (2004) argues, "universities must train students to work in Native communities, and offer fieldwork and courses that address contemporary Native issues and interests, as well as social, cultural, and political arrangements" (p. 35). Language, customs, songs, and traditions are important parts of communities and nations. Youth in these communities must know these things—where applicable—to participate as a member and citizen of their community or nation. They must also understand policies, rights, and the unique status of Indigenous peoples so that they can fully aid their communities and nations in the process of nation building. In short, combining tradition with policy work is an important part of nation building.

Conclusion

Nation building is a revolution of the spirit; it is a focused recommitment to traditional teachings (Alfred, 1999). Almost all models of Indigenous nation building seem to be in agreement that a project of nation building should be driven by the community, guided by an overall commitment to sovereignty (Alfred, 1999, 2005; Blain, 2010; Cook-Lynn, 2001; Helton, 2003/2004) and economic development (Cornell and Kalt, 1998, 2006, 2010). In this way, self-determination is manifested. Policies rooted in nation building must benefit the good of community (Helton, 2003/2004), must focus on the wellbeing of present and future generations, and, as the authors of this monograph we would also add, policies must be guided by the voices, practices, and worldviews of past generations, when appropriate (Champagne, 2004; Helton, 2003/2004; St. Germaine, 2008; Cornell and Kalt, 1998, 2006, 2010; Villegas, 2009). Nation building and all of its aspects (for example, economic development, educational development, legal/political realm, and so on) must be driven by goals of social justice and must benefit community, people, and the land over individual profit and material gain. Before proceeding to an examination of the literature on American Indians in higher education, we want to offer some caveats and cautions. Although we argue for a social justice and community-service orientation in a nation-building model, we are not suggesting that there cannot be some material gain; we are suggesting that a nation-building agenda is not driven by this interest as its primary/sole objective.

Nation building is not about rejecting all things Western. Alfred (1999) is useful here when he notes, "cultural revival is not a matter of rejecting all Western influences, but of separating the good from the bad and of fashioning a coherent set of ideas out of the traditional culture to guide whatever forms of political and social development—including the good elements of Western forms—are appropriate to the contemporary reality" (p. 28). Indeed, nation building relies on tradition and Indigenous ways of knowing, but not with a reckless zeal. We are arguing that this also contains a distinctly modern element. Again, Alfred (1999, p. 28) offers guidance when he writes, "we must be careful not to romanticize the past. Tradition is the spring from which we draw our healing water; but any decisions must take into account contemporary economic, social, and political concerns . . . peace is hopeful, visionary, and forward looking . . . peace is being [Indigenous], breaking with the disfiguring and meaningless norms of our present reality, and recreating ourselves in a holistic sense."

Formal education helps build a foundation needed for citizens of Indigenous nations to operate and to utilize formal governments in developing/pursuing goals that will benefit and serve community needs. Akoto (1992, p. iv) points out that "When parents and teachers opt for nation building, they commit themselves to a world vision or world order that complements their sense of cultural/historical awareness and their unique humanity . . . Nation building is predicated upon historical awareness and cultural consciousness. To engage in nation building, the leadership of the nation, cultural group or community, must work to counteract generations of miseducation and the consequent psychic dependency, defeatism, self hatred, misguided loyalties, and the inferiority complex" that has existed for too many years. We now turn our attention to the experiences of Indigenous students in institutions of higher education.

Postsecondary Access for Indigenous Students

AMERICAN INDIAN AND ALASKA NATIVE student opportunities for higher education are influenced by a complex web of factors that include socioeconomic status, life experiences, family expectations and responsibilities, culture, tribal education policies and practices, perceptions about the relevance of higher education for living and working in tribal communities, and goals for work and life beyond the degree. All of the above are constrained or mediated by K–12 school contexts, policies, and practices; discrimination and academic tracking; students' proximity to colleges and universities; postsecondary institution costs; admission requirements; and outreach and political policies based on the notion of who merits college education as enacted through financial aid, affirmative action, and accountability plans. This chapter offers an overview of the research and data on postsecondary access for American Indian and Alaska Native students and a discussion of cultural, political, and geographic factors that are unique to the experiences of Native students.

Improving postsecondary access for Indigenous students is a critical component of nation building. Ensuring a nation's well-being requires the strengthening of political, economic, social, cultural, and spiritual processes within communities. Individuals who seek the knowledge, skills, and social capital offered by institutions of higher education can play a role in these processes. Educational success is one prerequisite for political and economic success within tribal communities, and improving postsecondary access for Indigenous students is a crucial aspect of increased educational success among tribal nations.

Postsecondary Aspirations, High School Completion, and Academic Preparation

Consistent with a nation-building agenda, American Indian and Alaska Native students have high expectations for college. These high expectations, however, are not reflected in their ultimate college enrollment. The percentage of Native tenth graders who expect to complete a bachelor's degree increased dramatically between 1980 and 2002 from 41 to 76 percent (Institute of Education Statistics, 2004). The National Indian Education Study Part II (NIES II), conducted by the Office of Indian Education and the National Center for Education Statistics (NCES), found that when students in the fourth and eighth grades were asked about their educational goals, the majority in both grade levels reported that they will "probably go to college" (65 percent for fourth-grade students and 78 percent for eighth-grade students; Moran and Rampey, 2008, p. 15).

The NIES II report also compares the postsecondary aspirations of Native students attending high-density schools (where 25 percent or more of the students are AI/AN) to those attending low-density schools (where less than 25 percent of the students are AI/AN), as well as students attending both public and Bureau of Indian Education (BIE) schools. Native eighth-grade students attending high-density schools reported higher college aspirations (82 percent) than those attending low-density schools (74 percent), whereas Native eighth-grade students attending public schools reported higher aspirations for college (79 percent) than did students attending BIE schools (69 percent). In spite of the increase in Native students' college aspirations, critical components of getting to college include completing a high school degree, taking college preparatory courses, and knowledge about how to get to college, including completing college entrance examinations and understanding the financial-aid process (Cabrera and La Nasa, 2000).

High School Completion

One of the critical conditions of college-going is completing a high school diploma (Cabrera and La Nasa, 2000). Native students arguably have the lowest high school completion rates in the country. For this chapter, drop-out rates are reported according to the cumulative promotion index (CPI) developed by

TABLE 1

High School Graduation Rates by Race/Ethnicity for the Class of 2007

Race/Ethnicity	High School Graduation Rate
All Students	69 percent
American Indian/Alaska Native	51 percent
Latina/Latino	56 percent
African American	54 percent
Asian American/Pacific Islander	81 percent
White	77 percent

Source: EPE Research Center (2010).

Swanson (2004, 2009), which uses longitudinal data to track student progress from ninth grade through twelfth grade. According to Swanson, half of all Native students (51 percent) will complete a high school diploma, compared to 69 percent of students overall; see Table 1.

Calculations of high school completion rates for Native students are complicated by a number of factors, including the high transfer rate of Native students between schools (St. Germaine, 1995) and the fact that measures of high school completion do not include students who leave school before ninth grade. Statistics on Native students who have dropped out of school before ninth grade are not available nationally or at the state level, and few tribes or tribal education departments have the infrastructural capacity to track their students through K–12 education and beyond.

The factors that contribute to high school drop-out rates are complex. Research on Native drop out has documented how negative academic and/or social experiences that begin in the primary grades continue throughout school. For example, in 2004, 7 percent of Native public school students in kindergarten through twelfth grade were suspended from school (more than any other racial/ethnic group with the exception of African Americans), and Native students reported more school absences than any other student group (DeVoe and Darling-Churchill, 2008). Although the reasons for chronic absenteeism are complex, students who are not in school miss out on educational opportunities and grow further behind in academic subjects. Greg Marston, Hoopa Tribal Education Association Director, explained that he traced the high school drop-out rate of Hupa youth to the fourth grade, when some students begin to get behind in content areas, and without intervention, this often accumulates so that before the end of middle school, course work becomes overwhelming and students feel demoralized and leave school (personal communication, December 15, 2008).

Factors such as discrimination, low teacher expectations, and disproportionate tracking of Native students into vocational, non-college-preparatory courses also push some students to leave school before graduating (Chavers, 2002; Cleary and Peacock, 1997; Deyhle, 1992; Deyhle and Swisher, 1997; Faircloth and Tippeconnic, 2010; Ortiz and HeavyRunner, 2003; Wright, Hirlinger, and England, 1998). Deyhle's (1992) longitudinal ethnographic study of Navajo school dropouts found students' feelings of discrimination and rejection resulted in student mistrust and alienation from school. Cultural discontinuity and the absence of culturally responsive or affirming curricula are also factors that may result in depressed attendance, academic achievement, and motivation to stay in school (Campbell, 2007; Demmert, 2001; Castagno and Brayboy, 2008; McCardle and Demmert, 2006; Mohatt, Trimble, and Dickson, 2006).

Academic Preparation

Academic preparation is a critical predictor of developing early college aspirations, enrolling in college immediately after high school, and ultimately completing a postsecondary degree (Achieve, Inc., 2009; ACT, 2007; Adelman, 2002, 2006; Cabrera and La Nasa, 2000; Hossler, Schmit, and Vesper, 1998; King, 1996; Kirst and Venezia, 2004; Perna, 2005; St. John, 1991; Shireman, 2004; Stampen and Fenske, 1988). The academic rigor of a student's high school curriculum is more predictive of long-term educational attainment than family socioeconomic status, and is the single best predictor of college graduation (Adelman, 2006).

Mathematics courses are particularly important gateway courses for college going; taking Algebra I by eighth grade and completing high-level math courses in high school provide the strongest likelihood for college going (Adelman, 1999,

TABLE 2

Proportion of American High School Students Who Graduated with College-Ready Transcripts, 2003

Race/Ethnicity	Percent of Students with College-Ready Transcripts
All Students	36 percent
American Indian/Alaska Native	21 percent
Latina/Latino	22 percent
African Americans	25 percent
Asian Americans/Pacific Islander	46 percent
White	39 percent

Source: Greene and Forster (2003).

2002, 2006; Perna, 2005; Spielhagen, 2006). There are other implications for math courses as well; recent research has shown that students who do not take academically challenging courses in high school are not only less likely to attend or succeed in college, but they do not do as well in the workforce compared to their counterparts (Adelman, 1999; Achieve, Inc., 2009). Native college-going students not tracked into college-preparatory courses by high school have less choice about where they can begin college and are much more likely to spend time and tuition on remedial education before they can advance to courses that count for transfer and/or degree completion (Ortiz and HeavyRunner, 2003). It is significant, then, that national studies have shown that the majority of Native students who graduate from high school are the least likely of all student groups to have completed the core courses necessary for college eligibility and preparation (Greene and Forster, 2003; Planty, Bozick, and Ingels, 2006).

As shown in Table 2, among American Indian/Alaska Native students who finish high school, only 21 percent graduate with college-ready transcripts (Greene and Forster, 2003). With the use of data from the 1998 National Assessment of Educational Progress (NAEP) High School Transcript Study, Greene and Forster distinguish a college-ready transcript as one showing that the student received a high school diploma and completed the coursework required for meeting the minimum eligibility criteria for admission to a four-year institution: four years of English, three years of math, and two years each of natural science, social science, and a language other than English; see Table 2.

In a study by the NCES (Planty, Bozick, and Ingels, 2006), student transcripts from the Educational Longitudinal Study of 2002 were analyzed to provide nationally representative data about the graduating class of 2003–2004. In this study, four curricular tracks were identified: 1) academic concentration, 2) occupational concentration, 3) academic and occupational concentration, and 4) general curriculum. The curriculum for the "academic concentration," the minimum required for admission in a four-year college or university, matches the college-ready set of courses in the Greene and Forster (2003) study: four years of college-preparatory English, three years of math beyond algebra, three years of laboratory science, three years of social studies, and two years of a language other than English.

By comparison, the occupational concentration includes at least three courses in a specific job-preparation area, such as agriculture, business, trade and industry, technology, food service, or child care. The general curriculum requirements do not meet the criteria for either the academic or the occupational concentrations. As Table 3 highlights, compared to all other racial/ethnic groups, American Indian/Alaska Native students are the most likely to be enrolled in a general curriculum, and the least likely to complete credit hours in courses that were part of the academic concentration.

Clearly, high school completion and academic preparation must be strengthened if Indigenous communities hope to improve educational success and, therefore, advance their nation-building agendas.

Accelerated Learning Opportunities

From 2001 to 2010 the number of American Indian/Alaska Native seniors who left high school having completed an Advanced Placement (AP) exam more than doubled—from 2,199 in 2001 to 4,891 in 2010—and the number of Native seniors scoring a 3 or higher on an AP exam has more than doubled from 988 in 2001 to 2,195 in 2010 (College Board, 2011). Although Native student participation in AP is increasing and improving, American Indian and

TABLE 3

Percentage of High School Graduates in Academic, Occupational, or General Programs, Academic Year 2003–2004

Race/ethnicity	Academic Concentration	Occupational Concentration	Academic and Occupational Concentration	General Curriculum
American Indian/ Alaska Native	13 percent	15 percent	1 percent	71 percent
Latina/Latino	16 percent	13 percent	2 percent	69 percent
African American	17 percent	16 percent	5 percent	63 percent
Asian American/ Pacific Islander	40 percent	7 percent	2 percent	51 percent
White	29 percent	16 percent	3 percent	52 percent

Source: Devoe and Darling-Churchill (2008).

Alaska Native students continue to remain underrepresented in AP, and Native students score lower on all AP subject-area examinations compared to their White and Asian American/Pacific Islander peers (College Board, 2011; DeVoe and Darling-Churchill, 2008).

In an extensive review of research on accelerated learning opportunities in Indian country, Benally (2004) observed that schools serving large numbers of Native students offer few, if any, opportunities for accelerated learning, including AP, honors, and International Baccalaureate (IB) courses. Even when Native students attend schools offering a full range of AP courses, a small percentage of Native students actually participate (Benally, 2004). In 2010, only 14 percent took the exam, and less than half (45 percent) earned scores of 3 or higher (ACT, 2010a; College Board, 2011). A study by the National Center for Education Accountability found that "minority and low-income students who score a 3 or higher on the exam are much more likely to earn a college degree within five years of beginning college than comparable low-income and minority students" (College Board, 2011, p. 3).

Benally (2004) explains that the ability of rural, small, and tribally controlled schools to offer AP courses must be placed into the larger context of

Indian education, where educational resources in general are scarce or limited and there may be a greater concern about larger educational issues beyond whether or not students are taking AP courses. Schools serving large numbers of Native students tend to be in rural areas, where opportunities to participate in accelerated learning are extremely limited because of schools' insufficient resources for attracting appropriately qualified personnel, for providing adequate technology, and for maintaining the capacity to provide the full range of college preparatory courses (McDonough, McClafferty, and Fann, 2002; Pavel, 1999; Ward, 1995).

Rural high schools are increasingly offering AP courses on-line, and these may especially benefit self-directed students with familiarity with the Internet (Marcel, 2003). In one study of American Indian college access (Fann, 2005), high school students from rural reservation communities whose only access to AP courses was via the Internet described several challenges with taking their most academically rigorous courses without the benefit of an on-site teacher, classroom peer support, or adequate library and/or laboratory facilities. An exploratory study conducted by the Western Consortium for Accelerated Learning Opportunities found that a significant percentage of rural and low-income students either withdrew from on-line AP courses before completion, earned lower-than-average or failing grades in the course, failed to take the AP exam even after completing and passing the course, or passed the course and took the exam but did not score high enough to receive college credit (Marcel, 2003).

Consider also that access to a computer at home and Internet connectivity are unavailable to some Native students living on remote reservations or federal trust lands. In general, Indian country tends to have the areas least served by telecommunications and broadband in the United States. The national U.S. phone coverage is 98 percent, but it is only 69 percent on tribal lands, and as low as 40 percent on many reservations (Government Accountability Office [GAO], 2006). It is estimated nationwide that less than 10 percent of the Native population has high-speed broadband access (National Congress of American Indians Policy Research Center, 2007). An NCES (2005a) report on Internet access indicates that only 41 percent of Native students have Internet access at home and even fewer (13 percent) have broadband at home. Many Tribal governments do not have a shared network or email system for basic intergovernmental communications (Great Plains Tribal Chairman's Association, 2010).

The Internet is a valuable tool for enhancing learning and educational prospects; for searching for different colleges, especially those far from home; for learning about admissions requirements; downloading application materials; and actually applying to college (Venegas, 2007). Expedited use of the Free Application for Federal Student Aid (FAFSA) requires access to the Internet, and having limited access to the Internet places additional burdens on students' (and their families') ability to apply for federal financial aid and to search and apply for other sources of college scholarships and grant funding. Colleges and universities increasingly rely on the Internet for recruitment, and the majority of college application processes, admissions processes, and financial aid processes are conducted entirely on-line, placing Native students with limited access to the Internet at a further disadvantage in accessing higher education.

These relationships between technology, accelerated learning opportunities, and postsecondary access highlight why nation building must be deliberate and collective. The educational success of Indigenous youth relies in part on the technological and school-based opportunities available within their communities. Nation building is about strengthening all aspects of communities, and educational success is also about building stronger communities.

College Entrance Examinations

Standardized college admission tests, the fairness of which is highly contested—especially for students of color—continue to be used as shorthand for determining merit in college admissions (Beatty, Greenwood, and Linn, 1999; Card and Rothstein, 2007). Native high school students who are not on the academic track are less likely to receive information or encouragement from school counselors for college going, including information about taking college entrance exams (Fann, 2005). Moreover, high schools in rural areas (where Native students living on or near reservation or trust land communities typically reside) have fewer resources to offer extracurricular support such as

SAT/ACT test preparation. In some cases, students in rural communities must travel long distances to regional SAT/ACT test centers, placing an additional burden on families without adequate transportation. It is not surprising, then, that overall, low-income and students of color are less likely than other students to take college admission exams (Hossler, Schmit, and Vesper, 1998; Perna, 2005). The 2010 class of SAT test takers was the most diverse on record. More AI/AN students are taking the SAT than a decade ago, and their scores are rising slightly, following a nationwide trend (College Board, 2011). Still, Native students' scores are lower on the SAT than White students', and Native students experience barriers when taking the exam, partly because of more limited access to and participation in academically rigorous courses and accelerated learning opportunities such as AP and honors courses (Benally, 2004; DeVoe and Darling-Churchill, 2008). Table 4 shows the total mean composite SAT and ACT scores by race and ethnicity for 2008 college-bound seniors.

There is some variation between male and female students' SAT scores. The critical reading SAT scores for both genders are virtually the same (486 males and 482 females). Native males score higher on the math portion (573) compared to females (505), although females score higher on the writing section (472) compared to males (456).

Economic Conditions and Paying for College

Community poverty, unemployment, and the accompanying lack of social services present substantial barriers to higher education. Although there have been increases in employment rates and incomes for AI/AN people living on reservations, on average, on-reservation Native residents are the economically poorest group in the United States. In 2000, the annual per-capita income of American Indians residing on reservations was $7,942, compared to $21,587 for the total U.S. population (HPAIED, 2008). American Indian and Alaska Native peoples experience the highest levels of poverty (26 percent), compared to White (9 percent), Asian American (13 percent), Native Hawaiian/Pacific Islander (18 percent), Hispanic/Latino (23 percent), and Black/African American (25 percent) ethnic groups (DeVoe and Darling-Churchill, 2008). American Indians living

TABLE 4

Average SAT and ACT Scores by Race/Ethnicity, 2010

	SAT: Mean Scores			
	Critical Reading	Math	Writing	ACT Composite Scores
American Indian/ Alaska Native	484	488	465	19.0
Asian American/ Pacific Islander	517	595	528	23.4
Black or African American	428	427	417	16.9
Mexican or Mexican American	451	466	445	*
Puerto Rican	452	452	442	*
Other Hispanic, Latino, or Latin American	451	462	444	*
Hispanic				18.6
White	528	535	516	22.3
Total	497	514	489	21.0

Source: College Board (2011), ACT (2010b).

on reservations experience the highest poverty rates of all (39 percent). Although Native nations continue to develop economically, the emergence of their economic growth started at such low levels of income and employment that it will take decades for Native incomes to catch up to average U.S. levels (HPAIED, 2008). Cunningham, McSwain, and Keselman (2007, p. 16) explain that "poverty is not just an economic phenomenon; it is a cyclical condition that affects multiple generations and is often accompanied by a range of social problems—such as substance abuse, health problems, domestic violence, and high mortality rates—which greatly affect a person's ability and desire to pursue education." Hence, nation building is an effort focused around economic development, social conditions, health, cultural knowledge, and educational success.

Low family incomes and rising tuition cause many Native students to rely heavily if not completely on a variety of financial-aid sources to make college going possible. There is a direct relationship between family income and going to college (Baker and Vélez, 1996; Fitzgerald and Delaney, 2002; Heller, 1999; Paulsen and St. John, 2002; Spencer, 2002; Stampen and Fenske, 1988). The gap in college going between the lowest and highest income families has remained wide since 1970; students from high-income families are 32 percent more likely to go to college than similarly qualified students from low-income families (Fitzgerald and Delaney, 2002), and students from low-income families attend public four-year institutions at about half the rate of equally qualified students from high-income families. Family income also has a significant impact on college persistence. According to a research commissioned by The Pell Institute (Engle and Tinto, 2008), 60 percent of low-income, first-generation students leave college after their first year, a rate four times greater than their peers who had neither of these risk factors. Additionally, only 11 percent of low-income, first-generation students had earned a bachelor's degree in six years, compared to 55 percent of their more advantaged peers.

A major reason for this is unmet financial need—the difference between the cost of one year of education and the amount of aid and family contributions paid toward that cost—which is much higher for low-income families. The average unmet need to attend a public four-year university is $3,800 for low-income students, compared to $400 for high-income students (Advisory Committee on Student Financial Assistance, 2001). In comparison with other racial/ethnic groups, Native students were second only to African American students in their receipt of financial aid (85 percent and 92 percent, respectively; Snyder and Dillow, 2010). Although tribally affiliated American Indian students have an additional avenue of financial aid through their tribe, the amount of funding available at the tribal level varies widely, as do the rules for accessing these funds, creating additional layers of bureaucracy within an already cumbersome and complicated system (W. G. Tierney, Sallee, and Venegas, 2007). Having unmet financial need for college is a significant barrier to post-secondary enrollment and/or persistence for Native students, as is the lack of timely information about how to access sources of financial aid (Cunningham, McSwain, and Keselman, 2007; Guillory and Wolverton, 2008; W. G. Tierney, Sallee, and Venegas, 2007). We move now to a discussion of the role of schools and college counseling in determining student participation in academically rigorous courses and their opportunities for accessing college knowledge.

The Role of Schools and College Counseling

The K–12 school system functions as a gatekeeper to postsecondary education through practices and policies that disproportionally redirect poor and minority students to vocational and general education tracks (McDonough, 1997, 2004, 2005; Oakes, 1985; Oakes and Saunders, 2007). Academic preparation for higher education is predicated upon information about college requirements, access to preparatory courses, and school staff expectations about students' ability to attend college. The way schools structure curricular offerings, access to information about how to get to college, and college advising send powerful messages to students about their ability to attend college.

First-generation college-bound students whose parents did not have the opportunity to go to college must rely almost exclusively on counselors and school staff for all information about getting to college (McDonough, 1997, 2004, 2005). Student access to college counseling within schools, and counselor roles in channeling students into certain courses, determines the quantity and quality of information students receive about college options and their eligibility for four-year institutions (Freeman, 1997, 1999; McDonough, 1997, 2004, 2005). According to Hawkins (1993), African American and Hispanic students have consistently received poor counseling because counselors tend to focus on students who fit preconceived notions of who will be successful, and "overworked advisors . . . tend to present more limited college options" (p. 14). Moreover, access to counseling is often dictated by track placement; if students are not on the college track they do not receive information about college (McDonough, 2004, 2005; Oakes, 1985).

There is very little research on college counseling specific to serving American Indian and Alaska Native students. In a qualitative study conducted by

Fann (2005) of fifty-three American Indian junior and senior high school students living on reservation communities, students with college aspirations reported mixed experiences with high school counselors. Although some were supportive, far too many were simply indifferent. Students already enrolled in college preparatory courses reported greater access to counseling and encouragement for college. The majority of students in the study, who were not enrolled in college-track courses, reported negative or indifferent responses to their queries about college, or acknowledged expectations that school personnel would provide them with information about how to get to college. These students described how they were perpetually waiting to receive information about college, a particularly troublesome finding, because these students were juniors and seniors and the acquisition of college qualifications is a by-product of the early development of educational plans and timely access to information and resources.

Student agency in seeking college counseling is also a factor in gathering college information, but student agency may be thwarted by factors such as campus climate, perceived counselor attitudes toward Native students, perceptions about counselor willingness to help, access to counselor time, and basic informational savvy about the steps to take, questions to ask, and who to talk to. Shutiva (2001) writes that understanding Native students' values and beliefs is central to providing meaningful academic and career guidance. She suggests training for school counselors serving Native students addressing the unique tribal historical, cultural, and political issues validating the traditional and contemporary cultures of Native students.

School practices, such as the absence of culturally relevant or affirming curriculum, low teacher expectations, and inappropriate teaching methods, have been shown to affect the academic achievement and mobility of Native students negatively (Cleary and Peacock, 1997; Deyhle and Swisher, 1997; Wright, Hirlinger, and England, 1998). Cultural discontinuity between Native communities and public schools has oft been cited to explain Native student alienation from formal education and decreased academic achievement (Agbo, 2001; Castagno and Brayboy, 2008; Cleary and Peacock, 1997; Demmert, 2001; Deyhle, 1995, 1998; Deyhle and Swisher, 1997; Hunt and Harrington, 2008; Ledlow, 1992; Peshkin, 1997; Pavel, 1999; Reyhner, Lee, and Gabbard, 1993;

St. Germaine, 1995). Conversely, Native students who have access to culturally relevant curriculum, including tribal language, and possess positive identities as Native people are predicted to have higher grades, higher self-esteem, and are less likely to drop out of school (Campbell, 2007; Coggins, Williams, and Radin, 1997; Demmert, 2001; Deyhle, 1995, 1998; McCardle and Demmert, 2006; Ledlow, 1992).

Although factors such as high school graduation, academic rigor, and financial aid are important, they cannot be considered in the absence of historical, cultural, and political factors that influence American Indian college aspirations and access. In describing the Mohawk Education Project, Agbo (2001, p. 52) writes, "In principle, the policy of raising academic standards seems desirable. However, in circumstances where academic standards convey only political undertones . . . and do not carry grassroots implications, it becomes difficult for American Indian students to achieve at the same level as their European-American counterparts."

A well-established body of research has addressed the educational experiences for students of color and found that racist attitudes, assumptions, and practices of teachers and school counselors affect academic achievement and college pathways for students of color (Deyhle, 1992, 1995; Oakes, 1985, Oakes, Rogers, Lipton, and Morrell, 2002; McDonough, Korn, and Yamasaki, 1997; Solórzano, 1992; Villalpando and Solórzano, 2005). Differences in performances across groups reflect the historic and ongoing socioeconomic disadvantages, segregation, and discrimination, and it can also cause students of color to make unfavorable assessments of their educational abilities and prospects (Steele and Aronson, 1995). According to Villalpando and Solórzano (2005), the low percentages of African American, Latino, and American Indian students who are eligible for university admission can partly be explained by the cumulative effects of inadequate academic preparation, negative teacher expectations, and the tracking of students of color disproportionately into nonacademic, vocational courses, making access to college seem beyond reach for these students. Freeman (1999) asserts that culture matters in college going:

> *Although it could be argued that the influences on students to choose or not to choose college participation are similar across cultures, the*

depth of meaning (the perception of reality) each culture attaches to those influences differs. It is necessary for educational policy makers to recognize and accept that the idea that racial and cultural considerations are important both in researching topic areas and in developing solutions for different groups [p. 10].

The benefits of higher education as an important pathway to social and economic mobility, as it is conventionally perceived, may not be viewed similarly in Indigenous cultures (Brade, Duncan, and Sokal, 2003; Brayboy, 2002; Cornell, 1987; Cornell and Kalt, 1992, 2003; Kirkness and Barnhardt, 1991; G. H. Smith, 2000; Waterman, 2007). Despite the increasing need for Native professionals, tribally articulated needs for higher education are complicated by priorities for self-government, cultural preservation, economic development, and a long history of traumatic experiences with formal education. Additionally, some Native students question the relevancy of a college education, because few postsecondary institutions offer courses directly applicable to working for a tribe, such as tribal law and federal Indian policy, cultural resource management, Indian education, or tribal languages and courses on Indigenous language revitalization and preservation (Kirkness and Barnhardt, 1991; Martin, 2005).

Moreover, a university degree does not automatically confer social status in tribal communities as it does in middle-class society. Formal education is often at odds with traditional tribal education, values, and teachings (Brade, Duncan, and Sokal, 2003; Brayboy, 2005b; Cunningham, McSwain, and Keselman, 2007; Kirkness and Barnhardt, 1991; Grande, 2004; L. T. Smith, 1999; Waterman, 2007). Native students may also feel reluctant to move away from home, and feel "confused by conflicting messages to leave the reservation and be successful and maintain their traditional connection to the tribe, land, and culture" (Jackson and Smith, 2001, p. 41).

Jennings (2004) examined the role of Alaska Native leadership in negotiating not only accessible but relevant higher education programs for Alaska Natives, and urges readers to understand that the cultural milieu of students cannot be taken for granted as a variable within a larger set of characteristics.

Culture must be explored as part of a fundamental framework on which Native nations understand everything from the basis and purposes of the educational endeavor to organizational and individual behavior on behalf of that endeavor (Jennings, 2004). This distinction cannot be emphasized enough. "Opposing worldviews and different understandings of the function of education in society has been at the root of failed programs and inappropriate structural responses" (Jennings, 2004, p. 5).

Protective Factors and Promising Practices for Postsecondary Access

In addition to the multiple challenges we have outlined for access to postsecondary education for Indigenous students, it is also important to discuss the protective and promising factors that facilitate successful transitions to college. Families, communities, and tribal nations can and do play critical roles in this process. There are also some promising programs and practices around the country helping to facilitate American Indian and Alaska Native students' access to higher education.

Family Involvement

Not only is there an opportunity for partnerships between Native families and communities, schools, and postsecondary institutions to have an impact on Native college-goers' aspirations and preparation for college, there is a great need, as well. The role of parents in cultivating early expectations for college is critical. Research has shown that parental support and encouragement is one of the most important indicators of students' educational aspirations (Auerbach, 2002; Hossler, Braxton, and Coopersmith, 1989; Hossler, Schmit, and Vesper, 1998; McDonough, 1997; Stage and Hossler, 1989). Unfortunately, parents who have not had opportunities to attend college themselves have neither experience with the process of college preparation and college going, nor access to needed information. The negative legacy of Western education in Native communities, structural barriers, cultural barriers, and school environments perceived as unwelcoming make it difficult for some Native parents to help their children prepare for college.

In Native communities, students' lives are intertwined with the lives of their whole communities, the totality of which affects both risks and opportunities (Besaw and others, 2004). This can be a significant protective factor whereby extended family and kin relationships within Native communities mean that students can rely on parents, family members *and* other adults in the community as important allies in college going. The imperative for schools, postsecondary institutions, and tribal education programs is to find meaningful ways to involve families and community members in the college-going process while developing strategies for extending college outreach to families with children in elementary and middle school. Moreover, schools and postsecondary institutions should operate under a culturally responsive definition of *families* that is community inclusive, and seek consultation and collaboration with tribal education and social service entities in designing outreach.

Tribal Nation and Community Involvement

Even though the majority of American Indian high school students attend public schools en route to mainstream postsecondary institutions that are outside of tribal control, tribes can and do play an active role in the process of college going. When tribes control economic development, these efforts are more likely to be both successful and sustainable (Cornell and Kalt, 1992, 2003, 2006; HPAIED, 2008). When tribes control education, evidence suggests that American Indian students do better (Tippeconnic, 1999, 2000). When tribes take control of getting their students into college, the likelihood of increasing postsecondary access and persistence grows exponentially. Evidence of this can be found in the outcomes of students who attend tribally controlled colleges (American Indian Higher Education Consortium [AIHEC], 2001; Benham and Stein, 2003; Cunningham, McSwain, and Keselman, 2007) and in innovative college access services and programs being developed by tribes and Native communities across the country.

It is evident that Native nations and communities should continue to work with policy makers, schools, and postsecondary institutions to develop culturally responsive ways to support students' transitions to higher education communities. Successful tribal programs cultivate early expectations for higher education and provide a variety of support to increase students' academic achievement and knowledge about how to get to college, making college-going an ongoing process rather than an isolated event. Equally important, successful postsecondary preparation programs foster students' involvement in learning tribal languages and participating in tribal cultural/social/political activities, encouraging students to believe that they will not have to choose between their home communities and culture, and being a college student.

Postsecondary Outreach

Early-intervention programs focus on enhancing the college awareness and readiness of underrepresented students and their families early enough to impact college aspiration formation. Such programs have become an increasingly important part of institutional strategies at national, state, and local levels, particularly because the commitment to affirmative action has been reversed in a number of states (Swail and Perna, 2002). Many early-intervention programs serve students beginning in middle school, because it is well established that the earlier a student develops college aspirations, the more likely it is that the student will attend college. Outreach programs provide a "safety net for thousands of students who do not get the level of support, academic and social, within their current academic environments to become college ready" (Swail and Perna, 2002, p. 16).

TRIO programs nationwide serve approximately 4 percent Indigenous students (www.trioprograms.org) and this percentage is fairly consistent across all six TRIO programs (Educational Opportunity Programs, Talent Search, Student Support Services, McNair Post-Baccalaureate Achievement, Upward Bound, and Upward Bound Math and Science). It is imperative that more American Indians and Alaska Natives gain access to these programs. Nationwide, the GEAR UP program served 1,483,763 total students during the 2004–2005 year, and American Indians and Alaska Natives comprised 37,976 (James Davis, a team leader for GEAR UP, personal communication, January 9, 2006). During the last year, then, GEAR UP programs served approximately 2.6 percent AI/AN students. Both the TRIO and the GEAR UP programs have come under scrutiny by the U.S. Congress and their funding has been in jeopardy. It continues to be imperative that these programs serve students who need their services and that they meet the needs of more American

Indian and Alaska Native students. College Horizons is a precollege workshop specifically for Indigenous students. Over 85 percent of students participating in College Horizons received their bachelor's degree within five years of their high school graduation. According to their Web site, the five-day crash courses help students select suitable colleges, complete competitive applications, gain test-prep skills, and navigate financial aid and scholarship information. Additionally, according to their director, College Horizons currently serves "1,800 high school students and 500 college/college graduates" (Carmen Lopez, College Horizons director, personal communication, November 2, 2010). In 2010, College Horizons served 234 Indigenous students (enrolled tribal members only) who were currently either juniors or seniors in high school; these students came from twenty-six states and sixty-six tribal nations. Approximately 47 percent of the students were first-generation college students, and only 36 percent were men (Carmen Lopez, personal communication, November 2, 2010).

Native-American–Serving Early College High Schools

Early-college high schools (ECHS) for Native youth are emerging as especially promising models for Native student college preparation and access. Early colleges serve low-income, first-generation college-bound youth through small, personalized secondary schools where students earn an associate's degree (or up to 60 college credits) free of charge concurrently with their high school diploma. Early-college high schools for Native youth are unique among early colleges in that they include 1) enrollment of AI/AN students; 2) integration of local culture into school curriculum; 3) college courses taught in the school so that students do not need to leave their community; 4) an inclusive, open-admissions process; and 5) extensive family, tribal, and community engagement (Campbell, Egawa, and Wortman, 2003). Native-serving early colleges include extensive collaboration between school districts, tribes or urban Indian communities, and colleges or universities.

To date there are fifteen Native Early College High Schools in a consortium coordinated through the Center for Native Education at Antioch University. Native early colleges are located in seven states, mostly in the West. According to the Center for Native Education Fact Sheet (2009):

At many early colleges, Native student graduation rates have climbed to 100 per cent.

Students have made dramatic academic gains, demonstrating a proficiency level of up to 92 percent on state reading assessments.

Early-college students have earned up to forty-five college credits before graduating high school.

Daily school attendance has increased up to 92 percent at some early colleges.

College enrollment for Native students graduating from some early colleges is 400 percent higher than before enrolling in early college.

College enrollment has increased for adult community members as well. Some adults have taken computer, English, and math classes at their local early college.

Examples of this include the Effie Kokrine Charter High School (EKCS) in Fairbanks, Alaska, where students receive an educational experience "rooted in the social, political, economic and cultural contexts of Interior Alaska" (Barnhardt and Laughlin, 2005). The curriculum at EKCS immerses students in real-world projects and activities, organized around themes, such as family, cultural expression, health and wellness, outdoor survival, and applied technology (Barnhardt and Laughlin, 2005). At Klamath Early College High School of the Redwoods located on the Yurok Reservation in Northern California, students meet their foreign language requirement by learning Yurok and participate in hands-on educational and community service activities such as collecting water samples for the tribe's fisheries department, and documenting tribal history through interviews with elders. The NAYA Early College Academy in Portland, Oregon is another noteworthy example of blending academic rigor and college preparedness with local Native culture in an urban Indian community. Similar to other ECHS for Native Youth, the NAYA Academy has advocates that help students with issues outside of school that prevent academic success, such as living in poverty, substance abuse, juvenile justice, and moving back and forth between the reservation and the city (Hansen, 2008).

Concluding Thoughts

Barriers to higher education severely limit American Indian/Alaska Native students' choices for career pathways and opportunities for higher-paying jobs, while at the same time depriving Native nations of the important contributions—from sustained sovereignty to self-determination to social and economic development—that a college-educated workforce can provide. That so few Native students have the opportunity to go to college is also a loss to higher education, as classrooms, campuses, research, and teaching are deprived of Indigenous perspectives and talent. Finally, the nation as a whole loses, as do communities across the country and every sector of the workforce, because they consequently lack the intellectual, cultural, professional, and personal contributions and presence of Native people. We are in dire need of more research that examines the educational and social conditions at every point in the pipeline, so that we can better understand what prevents Native students from having equal access to higher education. Moreover, research is also needed to explore how successful postsecondary access models like early-college high schools for Native youth and innovative tribally designed programs can be mimicked in other schools and in other communities serving Native students. Through these kinds of efforts, we see how nation building and educational success go hand in hand to develop individuals who work for the betterment of their communities.

American Indian and Alaska Native College Students

AMERICAN INDIAN AND ALASKA NATIVE student attendance and persistence in institutions of higher education are well below the national averages. As with their access to higher education, Indigenous students' participation in higher education is shaped by multiple factors at the individual, familial, community, tribal, and national levels. This chapter reviews what the data tell us about American Indian/Alaska Native student participation in college. We examine enrollment and retention statistics, the nature of Indigenous students' experiences in predominantly White colleges and universities, and the role of tribal colleges and universities.

It is important to note that sweeping statements about the achievement levels and experiences of Indigenous students are inherently problematic because of significant differences between tribal nations, between urban and reservation communities, and between traditional and less traditional Indigenous students. Just as the nation-building efforts are not exactly the same from one tribal nation to the next, so too is there important variability between the experiences of various Indigenous students in higher education. We must not lose sight of this diversity, but we also need to understand better the patterns and trends related to AI/AN students in colleges and universities. Only then can those of us working in institutions of higher education support the goals and desires of students, communities, and nations.

Enrollment Patterns

Although American Indian and Alaska Native enrollment in higher education has more than doubled in the past thirty years—from 76,100 in 1976 to

TABLE 5

Percentage of Population Ages Eighteen–Twenty-Four Enrolled in College or University, 2006

Race/Ethnicity	Enrollment Rate
All students	37 percent
American Indian/Alaska Native	26 percent
Latina/Latino	24 percent
African American	33 percent
Asian American	58 percent
Native Hawaiian/Pacific Islander	39 percent
White	41 percent

Source: NCES (2005a, p. 108).

166,000 in 2002 (NCES, 2005a)—the incredibly small overall numbers and percentages of Native students in higher education demonstrate the imperative for more research on Indigenous students' participation in postsecondary education. American Indian and Alaska Native students between the ages of eighteen and twenty-four remain less likely to be enrolled in a college or university than their White, Asian Pacific American, or Black/African American peers (DeVoe and Darling-Churchill, 2008). Table 5 shows the number of AI/AN students enrolled in college in 2006. Only 26 percent of American Indian/Alaska Native eighteen–twenty-four-year-olds were enrolled in college, compared to 37 percent of the total population.

In the past thirty years, college enrollment for American Indian/Alaska Native male and female students grew at different rates. In 1976, the number of AI/AN males and females was nearly equal; however, by 2006, there were 111,000 AI/AN females (61 percent of all AI/AN students) enrolled in higher education compared to 71,200 males, or 39 percent of the total (Knapp, Kelly-Reid, and Ginder, 2008, p. 159). There is a dearth of research addressing the particular needs and experiences of Native males in regards to college access or persistence and, as we have suggested elsewhere (Brayboy, 2010), health care, employment, and other economic issues may figure into the growing gender gap in male and female college attendance.

In addition to examining the general enrollment patterns for Indigenous students, educators and policy makers must also consider the types of institutions in which students are enrolled. There clearly exists a hierarchy among institutions of higher education, and some types of institutions only offer degrees in particular fields or up to a particular level. As Lowe (2005, p. 34) notes, "little has changed with respect to the types of institutions at which Native American students are enrolled. Data show that Native Americans continue to be underrepresented both in the more prestigious private and four-year sectors of higher education and over-represented in the less prestigious public and two-year sectors."

Native students are more likely to attend two-year colleges than four-year institutions (Cunningham, McSwain, and Keselman, 2007; DeVoe and Darling-Churchill, 2008; Pavel, 1999; Pavel and others, 1998; Pewewardy and Frey, 2002). This is not surprising given issues of proximity to four-year institutions, high school academic preparation, and socioeconomic status. Low-income students tend to aspire to less selective institutions than middle- and high-income students with comparable academic records (McDonough, Korn, and Yamasaki, 1997), and they are less likely to enroll in their first choice of institution (Hurtado, Inkelas, Briggs, and Rhee, 1997; Perna, 2000). Students who enroll in four-year institutions at the outset are more likely to complete degrees than those who enroll in two-year colleges (Astin and Oseguera, 2004; Bowen and Bok, 1998). Although two-year colleges remain the most financially, geographically, and academically accessible routes to higher education for nontraditional, minority, and rural students (Cohen and Brawer, 2003; Rosenbaum, Deil-Amen, and Person, 2006; Townsend, 1997), only 22 percent of students who start at the community colleges with intentions to transfer actually do so (Cohen and Brawer, 2003). Table 6 shows the enrollment patterns of Native students across institutional types.

These data may be indicative of the type of education that Indigenous students are receiving. The point here is not to make judgments about the quality of public education, but to highlight the limited access to more private, elite institutions. The fact that students of color are more apt to attend larger, less well-funded schools is clearly articulated by Swail, Redd, and Perna (2003). Indigenous students comprise 87 percent, compared with 78 percent of all

TABLE 6

Percentage of AI/AN Enrollment by Institutional Type, 2006–2007

	Two Year	Public, Four Year	Private, Not for Profit	For profit	Other
AI/AN	45.8 percent	31.1 percent	6 percent	5.3 percent	11.8 percent
All under-graduates	40.7 percent	30 percent	13.5 percent	7.8 percent	8 percent

Source: NCES (2005b).

students, who attend two-year and public institutions (Swail, Redd, and Perna, 2003). In 2008, 21 percent of White, 18 percent of Asian/Pacific Islander, and 17 percent of Black students attended private not-for-profit institutions, while 11 percent of Hispanic and 12 percent of AI/AN students did so (NCES, 2010). According to the NCES Higher Education General Information Survey (NCES, 1998), between 1976 and 1996 the numbers of AI/AN students in private institutions increased from 0.4% to 0.6%—up 50% from 8,600 to 17,700. Although any increases in the numbers of Indigenous students are promising, we still do not see equitable representations of Indigenous students in more elite institutions of higher education.

Retention Patterns

Once enrolled in institutions of higher education, AI/AN students experience the lowest graduation rates among all racial/ethnic groups. Whereas 4 percent of the Indigenous population in the United States has a bachelor's degree, 27 percent of the White population holds this degree (Native American Higher Education Initiative, 2005). In other words, for every one American Indian or Alaska Native who has a bachelor's degree, seven White individuals do. This number is stunning, given the economic, political, and social benefits that accrue for college-educated individuals in U.S. society. When measured according to six-year graduation rates, retention gaps exist between Indigenous students and their peers. See Table 7.

TABLE 7

Six-Year Graduation Rates

	Six-Year Graduation Rates for AI/AN Beginning College in 1996–1997
American Indian/Alaska Native	36.7 percent
Latina/Latino	38.2 percent
African American	44.8 percent
Asian American/Pacific Islander	62.6 percent
White	57.2 percent

Source: NCES (2005b).

Compared to White students, the graduation rates are lower for students of all underrepresented groups, except Asian Americans/Pacific Islanders. American Indian and Alaska Native students have the lowest aggregate graduation rate among all racial/ethnic groups; Indigenous men are less likely to graduate than Indigenous women: the six-year graduation rate for AI/AN men from the 1996–1997 academic year is 34.3 percent, compared to 38.6 percent for AI women (NCES, 2005a).

The enrollment of AI/ANs in institutions of higher education has increased significantly in the past thirty years, but as we noted above, AI/AN women have experienced a significantly higher increase in enrollment over AI/AN men. A similar pattern holds for the distribution of degrees during the past thirty years. Table 8 illustrates the change in degree distribution for AI/AN men and women between the years 1976 and 1994. For example, among AI/AN students, female bachelor degree recipients increased 135 percent between 1976 and 1994, whereas male bachelor degree recipients increased by just 51 percent during those same years. Likewise, female doctoral degree recipients increased by 143 percent, whereas male doctoral degree recipients *decreased* by 0.1 percent during those years. A similar pattern of higher rates of degree distribution holds for all degree levels.

As indicated in Table 8, the trend for American Indian men is distressing, particularly when examining the fact that American Indian men are receiving fewer doctoral degrees now than they were thirty years ago. This decrease indicates a crisis that must be addressed. Nation building among tribal nations

TABLE 8

Percent Change in Degree Distribution Between 1976 and 1994

Type of Degree	AI Women	AI Men
All degrees awarded	135 percent	45 percent
Associate	137 percent	51 percent
Bachelor	135 percent	45 percent
Master	126 percent	33 percent
Doctorate	143 percent	−0.1 percent
Professional	303 percent	40 percent

Source: Pavel, and others (1998).

requires both men and women who pursue higher education in order to develop and sustain healthy communities, institutions, and knowledge.

The Experiences of Indigenous College Students in Predominantly White Institutions

Overall, the literature about retention and persistence of Indigenous college students points to a number of factors related to their success and failure. Consistent with studies of persistence for other underrepresented groups, a number of studies argue that AI/AN postsecondary persistence is positively related to involvement in culture-related extracurricular activities (Hoover and Jacobs, 1992), relations with faculty who have an understanding of Indigenous cultures and histories (Reyhner, 1997), and financial support from either personal or institutional sources (McNamara, 1982). In their interviews with 125 Indigenous college students, Falk and Aitken (1984) found that support from family and the larger Native community, adequate academic preparation in multiple subject areas, institutional support services, increased access to financial aid, and adequate personal motivation on the part of the student were all related to higher levels of AI/AN student retention. Bowker's (1992) study of Indigenous women's educational experiences found the strongest relationships between Native women's departure from postsecondary institutions and their poverty, their lack of a strong sense of ethnic identity (either identifying with the Indigenous or White culture), pregnancy, fear of acting White, and racism.

Given the extremely low rates of enrollment and graduation, it should not be surprising that much of the research describing the state of Native America in college centers on either explaining why the graduation rates are low or outlining prescriptions for fixing the problem. Most of this research focuses on the individual student. However, there is some work that focuses on both the student and the larger structural barriers that influence the experiences of Indigenous college students. This work moves away from locating the lack of academic success in the student and instead examines the role of the institution and larger American society in the problems encountered by Indigenous students. In what follows, we review both sets of scholarship.

The higher education literature relies on a few main theories for explaining student participation in colleges and universities. Although W. Tierney (1992) and others have criticized the use of Tinto's (1975, 1986) model of student departure in scholarship on Indigenous higher education, the model continues to be used. But there are at least two alternative models developed to explain Indigenous students' experiences in institutions of higher education specifically. HeavyRunner and DeCelles (2002) developed the family education model (FEM) to explain student retention for Indigenous students better than more traditional models (i.e., Tinto's theory of student departure, Astin's theory of involvement, and Pascarella's general model for assessing change). The FEM is Indigenous based and suggests that universities ought to recreate the extended family structure within institutional settings in order to enhance Indigenous students' feelings of belonging and support. McAfee (1997, 2000) offers another model, and her work reminds us that statistics about degrees earned may be unreliable because the majority of Indigenous college students will have at least one "stepping out" experience some time in their college career. She uses the concept of *stepping out* rather than *dropping out* because she argues it is more accurate to portray Indigenous college attendance in terms of stepping stones; those that were successful and eventually earned a degree in her study were able to find the needed stepping stones to navigate the institution. "Each stepping stone is identified with positive factors that kept students in school or brought them back into higher education, and with negative factors that served to pull them out and kept them disengaged from higher education . . . However, no particular stepping stone is singularly necessary and sufficient for the participants [in her research] to remain in school" (McAfee, 2000, p. 3). The stepping stones she identifies are cultural identity, academic preparation, financial resources, motivation, family support, academic performance, alcohol and drug use, and institutional interface; she notes that cultural identity was the most prominent factor that emerged from her research.

At the heart of these issues is the manner in which institutions operate and the ways in which classrooms are run. Is there room in institutions for students who quietly do their work? Are there different ways to negotiate the institution and maintain a connection to other cultural ways of being? Most qualitative studies agree that students can accommodate. The more important piece to arise from an examination of these studies is whether or not institutions can do thorough, honest assessments of their campus climates. Are the institutions hostile to other ways of thinking and interacting? Is the institution welcoming to divergent viewpoints, and is there a place for Indigenous students to engage in schooling in ways that are comfortable for them?

As we have been suggesting, institutions of higher education must provide culturally responsive schooling that is grounded in Indigenous knowledge systems, sovereignty, and nation building. Education must be relevant to the current issues and struggles facing Indigenous students and communities, and it must provide opportunities for Indigenous students to learn about the policies, rights, and status of Indigenous peoples and nations in the United States. This would demonstrate a commitment by mainstream institutions to ensure higher education for nation building.

Cultural Differences

The differences between life at and in universities and at home on reservations, urban areas, or other highly concentrated pockets of Indigenous people can be dramatic. The differences between these lives is, perhaps, the most studied area in educational research on Indigenous students (Carroll, 1978; Lin, LaCounte, and Eder, 1988; Scott, 1986; St. Germaine, 1995). Many scholars draw on cultural-difference theories for understanding the low educational attainment of students of color at predominantly White colleges. Watson, Terrall, Wright, and Associates (2002), for example, found that the "notions of the ideal institutional environment" for minority students was "often at odds with many traditional institutional environments." Similarly, a common theme in the literature about Indigenous students in mainstream institutions of higher education is the overwhelming cultural discontinuity that often exists between the Native students and the culture of the institution. The stories compiled from Indigenous graduates of Dartmouth illustrate the dissonance felt by many students (Garrod and Larimore, 1997). From learning the correct way to make appointments with college administrators (Bray, 1992), to hearing harshly spoken words (Worl, 1992), to setting aside cooperation for individualism and competition (N. Adams, 1992), there are often multiple and various cultural differences between Indigenous students and mainstream universities.

Other scholars focus on the competing worldviews and conceptions of legitimate knowledge and argue that these differences impact how Indigenous students experience college (Brown, 2000; Carney, 1999; Fixico, 1995). Fixico (1995), for example, notes the following:

> In the educational process of American Indian students attending mainstream schools, students are compelled to understand or perceive everything from the mainstream point of view. But the instructor should be cognizant that traditional Indian youths also possess a Native perspective that is likely incongruent with mainstream thinking. For these students, they are learning in an alien culture. This unacknowledged and unaccounted for conflict between perspectives has resulted in many Indian students doing poorly in school and dropping out [pp. 108–109].

According to Fixico, and others, our schools fail to recognize how Indigenous students' perceptions, values, and worldviews might be different from those of the majority. In a similar vein, Gilmore, Smith, and Kairaiuak (1997) argue that "the institution views students as individuals; the students, in contrast, view themselves as part of a connected web of family and community" (p. 95). They go on to describe how the incompatible notions about the very nature and purpose of higher education cause clashes between Indigenous students and the institution. As an example, they explain how "the need to separate facts from values or feelings and to make decisions on the basis of facts alone" is one of the tenets of the positivism that characterizes Western institutions (Gilmore, Smith, and Kairaiuak, 1997, p. 95). Unfortunately, they argue, this epistemology "seriously clashes" with the Alaska aboriginal society in which they conducted their research.

We learn, then, that multiple and fundamental cultural discontinuities exist between many Indigenous students' cultures and the culture of their college or university. Some scholars believe that this cultural dissonance is especially prevalent for Indigenous students. Because some AI/AN students come to the university after having spent their entire childhood in a community of Indigenous people separated from the mainstream White community, the likelihood that these students will experience more acute cultural differences is high.

But we should not lose sight of the diversity among Indigenous students. Most of the available research is based on AI/AN students from rural or reservation communities. The studies talk about the cultural dissonance felt by these students and make it seem as if *all* Indigenous students are coming from these more traditional backgrounds. Although this research is extremely important, it seems to ignore the experiences of students who are from urban or suburban predominantly White communities. In *American Indians and the Urban Experience*, Lobo and Peters (2001) argue that limited information exists about urban Indigenous peoples because of the widespread assumption that Native people reside in rural settings and the tendency of academics (and especially anthropologists) to focus on rural communities. This argument is important to keep in mind in analyses of Indigenous participation in institutions of higher education because significant numbers of students are coming from these communities and are often more assimilated than the extant literature would have us believe. In two different qualitative studies of Indigenous students in colleges, for example, students indicated a range of identities among Indigenous students—some of whom were very assimilated or less culturally connected, and others who were very much connected to their tribal nations and cultures (Brayboy, 1999; Castagno, 2003).

Thus, there are a number of issues commonly cited as potential pitfalls for Indigenous students' successful negotiation of institutions of higher education (IHEs). First, AI/ANs are often viewed as placing a premium on cooperation when competition is valued in universities. Individually centered students do well at universities, but many Native students are more community centered; hence, they do not perform as well as non-Indigenous students. Indigenous students tend to fare well in small-group settings or in one-on-one encounters; at most universities these types of interactions are limited. More recently, Brayboy (1999, 2004, 2005b) and Waterman (2007) have found that those students who are focused on completion so that they can give back to their communities are more successful in completing college than their peers who are focused solely on themselves and individual achievement. Those students who are trained to be aggressive and orally combative fare well in some university settings. The academic aggression necessary to succeed is anathema to many Indigenous ways of being, so many students resort to silence in classrooms. Ultimately, the price of silence is great among Indigenous students. There is contradictory evidence that shows that students who are more traditional or bicultural do worse in college because of the incongruities (Carroll, 1978), and others who argue that these students actually perform better in schools (Brayboy, 2004, 2005b; Kirkness and Barnhardt, 1991). Either way, the campus context is an important factor in how Indigenous students experience and negotiate postsecondary education.

Campus Context

Tierney (1992) characterizes Indigenous student experiences in higher education as "official encouragement and institutional discouragement." Despite positive rhetoric, many mainstream universities are not hospitable places for Indigenous students (Bass, 1971; Benjamin, Chambers, and Reiterman, 1993; Houser, 1991; Kahout and Kleinfeld, 1974; Kirkness and Barnhardt, 1991; Pavel and Colby, 1992; Woodcock and Alawiye, 2001; Wright, 1990a). The campus climate is shaped by many factors, but there are a handful of studies that focus specifically on how campus context and climate relate to Indigenous students.

Guillory and Wolverton (2008) compared Indigenous students' perceptions with the perceptions of university faculty and administrators regarding the barriers and facilitators to persistence. Through interviews with thirty students and fifteen faculty and administrators at three different public universities in the western United States, these authors found that although the faculty and administrators identified financial support and academic programs and preparation as the primary persistence factors affecting Indigenous students, the students identified family, giving back to their tribal communities, and on-campus social support as key persistence factors and family, single parenthood, lack of academic preparation, and inadequate financial support as core barriers to persistence. Although we have concerns about these authors' interpretation of some of the data they present—particularly around failing to identify deficit models within some of the faculty and staff interview data—their general point regarding the "somewhat contrary views" between students and faculty and administrators is illuminating and important (Guillory and Wolverton, 2008, p. 80). Waterman's (2007) research with 12 Haudenosaunee college graduates reveals that the average time needed by her participants to complete a four-year degree averaged nearly eight years. She also notes that high school guidance counselors provided little help to these students, most of whom navigated the college application and financial aid processes alone and with the help of their families. Community college was an important "mediating experience" for almost all of these students, particularly for those who did not have a high school diploma and those who needed to raise low grade-point averages from earlier years in college. The social support for Indigenous students in Waterman's study came primarily from Native friends and family and their home communities, and they all maintained cultural integrity by "remaining centered in their culture, community, and family" (Waterman, 2007, p. 31). These studies help us better understand the campus experience for some American Indian and Alaska Native students; they also highlight how patterns in high school regarding lack of counseling support and the importance of culturally responsive schooling are relevant in the higher education context as well.

Recently, the National Collegiate Athletic Association (NCAA) issued a motion to remove all Indigenous mascots from institutions of higher education; sanctions were attached to the failure to justify the use of these mascots. Many institutions with these mascots and their alumni were vehement in their response to the NCAA's requirement. Several institutions have appealed, and some have been granted a waiver; others have not. In an era when individuals in the United States drive Cherokees, Dakotas, and Pontiacs, and when the U.S. Congress is disheartened by the loss of a Kiowa, Comanche, Blackhawk, or Apache attack helicopter, there appears to be little attention paid to the lives of the Cherokee, Dakota, Kiowa, or Apache peoples. The American Psychological Association recently released a statement regarding the use of American Indian mascots and symbols; they argued that the use of these symbols was not only detrimental to the education and well-being of Indigenous people, but also to society at large. Citing empirical studies, the statement argued that institutions should move away from the use of these mascots and symbols because of the detrimental effects on the lives of students and citizens in general. Issues of climate include, but are not limited to, the use of Indigenous mascots and symbols.

Other research has pointed to the prevalence of racism and policies inconsistent with the goal of supporting Indigenous students across college campuses (Castagno and Lee, 2007; Pewewardy and Frey, 2002, 2004). Kirkness and Barnhardt (1991) address the ways that colleges and universities continue to perpetuate policies and practices that historically produced abysmal graduation rates for American Indian students. Their work focuses on institutional discrimination and racism that presents barriers to American Indian academic success. Brayboy's (2004, 2005b) work highlights the ways that American Indian Ivy League college students used strategies that enable them to be academically successful. He examines the notion of visibility and the ways that structures can be both constraining and enabling. Importantly, American Indian and Alaska Native Studies programs on mainstream campuses have provided spaces that offer more culturally relevant environments for Indigenous students. This is an important development in the last thirty-five years, but does not excuse mainstream universities from making changes.

Paying for College

Indigenous youth disproportionately come from economically poor families and require financial assistance to pursue higher education (Cunningham, McSwain, and Keselman, 2007). A report published in 2007 concludes that there are insufficient funds for Indigenous students to pay for postsecondary education, and that many Indigenous students fear that they will incur too much debt if they rely on loans to fund their higher education goals (Tierney, Sallee, and Venegas, 2007). Tierney, Sallee, and Venegas (2007) highlight the complexity of financial aid issues for Indigenous students:

> *About 68 percent of American-Indian students receive some form of financial aid—either a grant or a loan. . . . American Indian students rank second in overall receipt of aid awards; they surpass the national average of students who receive aid by 4.3 percent. While this seems to be good news, a closer look at the amount of aid that students received suggests otherwise. The national average amount of federal or state aid is $6,892 per student. For American Indian students, the average amount of financial aid awards is $6,413, ranking fourth out of the five categories of racial/ethnic groups. There is a difference of $479 between the average aid received and the average aid received by American Indians. One semester of full-time tuition is $479 for community colleges in New Mexico, or up to 25 percent of community college or regional four-year college tuition rates in states like Montana and Arizona. These gaps in funding can make the difference in deciding whether or not to pursue postsecondary education [p. 19].*

Thus, despite the widespread assumption that Indigenous students have access to plenty of funding to finance higher education, this is more myth than reality. We see that this is not actually the case. Even for students who successfully navigate the complicated processes of applying for federal, state, and tribal monies, the average amount may not cover their expenses.

The unemployment and poverty rates for AI/ANs is particularly troubling as states move more toward merit-based rather than need-based financial assistance. According to St. John (1991, 2004), over the last twenty years tuition rates have skyrocketed and the purchasing power of federal Pell grants has declined by more than half. In response, many states have implemented merit-based grant programs to streamline their available moneys to students who meet certain merit criteria. Much research has shown that although these programs improve college access for White students and students from middle-income backgrounds, they do not have similar results for students of color. Further, states have not made comparable investments in need-based grants to equalize opportunity for poor and working-class students. In addition, Heller (2005) points to the fact that many merit-based financial aid programs often benefit students who may have attended institutions of higher education without aid. In fact, in Georgia, over 90 percent of the expenditures went to students who would have attended college anyway and actually increased the gap in college participation between White and Black students. In Florida and Maine, grants were awarded disproportionately to White students and students from wealthier communities (i.e., those students who already have higher participation rates in college). Ultimately, calls for more merit-based aid help many individuals who do not necessarily need it and hurt individuals who are most in need.

Aside from privately funded scholarship programs, Indigenous students potentially have access to federal, state, and tribal monies to support postsecondary education. It is important, therefore, that we better understand what these forms of support generally look like. Federal aid often comes in the form of much larger loan amounts than grant amounts—leaving potential students wondering if they will be able to repay money borrowed if they decide to pursue a degree. State aid varies drastically depending on where a student lives, but most of the states with the highest populations of Indigenous people rank toward the bottom in terms of their ability to provide student aid that meets anticipated student need. Variation also exists between the funding available from different tribal nations, but many of the largest tribes process far more applications for aid than they are able to fill in any given year (Tierney, Sallee, and Venegas, 2007).

Some critics have argued that Indigenous students do not need financial assistance to attend college because their tribal nations already receive income from both casino revenue and the federal government. This argument, however, is seriously flawed because it fails to recognize the heterogeneity in both sources of income between tribal nations. Table 9 illustrates some of the discrepancies by comparing the casino revenue and federal aid available to members of various tribal nations.

TABLE 9

Casino Revenue and Federal Aid for Members of Various Tribal Nations

Tribal Nation	Total Population	Casino Revenue per Member	Federal Aid per Member
Navajo	260,010	$0	$912
Hopi	11,267	$0	$2,006
Mississippi Choctaw	8,823	$25,048	$5,717
Seminole	2,817	$87,682	$8,540
Mashantucket Pequot	677	$1,624,815	$2,304
Miccosukee	400	$250,000	$20,560
Santa Ynez	159	$1,257,862	$8,360

Source: Bartlett and Steele (2002).

Clearly, blanket arguments about the "advantages" accrued through Indian gaming are uninformed. Furthermore, as *Indian Country Today* has noted, "Indian gaming is self-reliance" and has created over 300,000 jobs nationwide—many of which go to non-Indigenous employees of the gaming industry (J. Adams, 2002; Stevens, 2002). Casinos on tribal lands thus benefit a range of constituencies, because tribal nations have numerous service agreements with other tribal nations to support their endeavors and with state and local governments to share revenue and provide infrastructure support. Still, however, the presence of these casinos on some tribal nation lands does not mean that Indigenous students as a whole are financially able to support themselves through the attainment of a higher education.

Tribal Colleges and Universities

In addition to mainstream colleges and universities, tribally controlled institutions of higher education play a significant role in the educational attainment of Indigenous students. Most tribal colleges and universities (TCUs) are operated and run by tribal nations. However, two of the tribal colleges (Haskell Indian Nations University and Institute of American Indian Arts) are operated by Native peoples, but run by the Bureau of Indian Education (BIE), part of the U.S. Department of Interior. In many ways, TCUs are an exception in regards to American Indian and Alaska Native postsecondary participation. TCUs have a unique institutional capacity for promoting tribal students' academic success, transfer, and four-year degree completion (AIHEC, 1999, 2000, 2001; Benham and Stein, 2003; Cunningham, McSwain, and Keselman, 2007; Gonzalez, 2008; Pavel, Inglebret, and Banks, 2001; Stein, 1992, 1999). TCUs play a critical role in tribal workforce development and, because of their location on reservations in areas far removed from other college opportunities, provide postsecondary access to many students who would otherwise not be able to attend.

Tribal colleges and universities serve as a major destination for Indigenous students entering higher education. After a two-year campaign, TCUs became land-grant institutions through a 1994 Act of Congress. This status was awarded as part of the Elementary and Secondary Educational Act (ESEA). This bill also authorized a $23 million endowment from which TCUs would receive interest payments each year for operating costs and student scholarships. The role of tribal colleges and universities in the experiences of Indigenous students in higher education has, until recently, been missing from the research literature. We believe, however, that the role of these institutions will become more central to examining the experiences of AI/ANs in higher education. We also believe that other IHEs will need to examine and explore what TCUs are doing to meet the needs of their students and utilize these strategies as a blueprint for their own institutions.

There are currently thirty-six TCUs in the United States, the majority of which are chartered by their own tribal government, each offering courses and training that meet the particular development needs of the reservation community (AIHEC, 1999, 2000, 2001). Eight percent of AI/AN college students are enrolled in a tribal college (DeVoe and Darling-Churchill, 2008). TCUs are located in fourteen states—the majority in the west and midwest, with one in Alaska. Seven of the colleges and universities are four-year institutions and twenty-nine are two-year institutions. Most if not all TCUs collaborate with regional universities and/or other community colleges through distance education and articulation agreements, offering students access to additional courses and advanced degrees. TCUs also provide critically needed services to support the surrounding community, such as libraries, health care facilities, support for entrepreneurial and economic development, and cultural preservation projects (AIHEC, 2000, 2001). Enrollment in TCUs range from a couple hundred students to a few thousand, and the proportion of Indigenous students in the overall enrollment at each TCU varies from 60 to 100 percent (Snyder and Dillow, 2010).

The Kellogg Foundation, which invested $30 million in American Indian and Alaska Native higher education between the mid-1990s and early 2000s, notes that, "together, the Native-controlled colleges represent the most significant and successful development in Native American educational history. Their unique blend of quality education with Native American culture and values promotes achievement among students who may never have known educational success, but who are now emerging as leaders, cultural intermediaries, and changemakers" (Native American Higher Education Initiative, 2005, p. 2). According to a report commissioned by the Kellogg Foundation, "policy efforts, such as the Executive Order on Tribal Colleges and Universities, signed in 1998, have also led to emerging funding opportunities with various federal agencies" (American Indian College Fund, 2004, p. 4). Additionally, TCUs "have increased efforts to work together with other diverse higher education institutions, particularly Historically Black Colleges and Hispanic-Serving Institutions, to help shape national agendas and collaborate for the common good. For example, these three groups of institutions joined forces for the first time by forming the Alliance for Equity in Education for the purpose of informing policymakers about common concerns" (American Indian College Fund, 2004, p. 5).

There is clearly some evidence that TCUs are making a difference for both individual students and for their communities. A 1983 American Indian Higher Education Consortium (AIHEC) study found a 75 percent greater completion rate for AI/AN students who completed a course of study at TCUs and then continued on to a four-year degree program than among AI/AN students who went directly to four-year institutions. Surprisingly, there have not been any follow-up studies to further examine these rates of completion. We also know that about 85 percent of tribal college graduates who remain on reservations were employed (Pavel, 1998). Hill (1991) has argued that one in every four jobs on tribal lands is held by a non-Indigenous person, most of which are professional jobs that require college degrees. Thus, if TCUs can educate tribal nation citizens and have them stay on their tribal lands or prepare them to work with Indigenous communities, the institutions are meeting the needs of many. In this way, TCUs are engaging in their own form of nation building. Although TCUs are meeting many of the needs of reservation and rural Indigenous communities, there is still much work to be done.

There is also some evidence that relying solely on TCUs to educate Indigenous peoples in the United States may be problematic. A recent study of the enrollment and graduation patterns of 1,135 tribal college students who studied at the Fort Berthold Community College (FBCC) on the Fort Berthold Indian Reservation in New Town, North Dakota between 1987 and 1995 found that by spring of 1997, only 232 students (20 percent) received either a two-year degree or nine-month certificate as their first degree (Patterson, 2002). This study identified tribal affiliation, full-time student status, and higher levels of financial aid as factors that contributed to higher rates of degree completion among tribal college students. Although tribal colleges and universities clearly play an important role in improving the educational attainment and economic development of tribal nations, the larger higher education community must also work with these institutions to ensure equitable access to all postsecondary institutions.

Conclusion

Viewed through the lens of nation building, it is clear that Indigenous student participation in higher education is an issue that tribal nations, Native communities, families, and institutional leaders must address. There are significant challenges facing Indigenous students who want to enroll in and complete college. There are few Indigenous role models, which is a pattern likely to continue unless the initial college-going and completion rates are not addressed immediately. The cultural differences between institutions are intense and, in some cases, counterproductive. Without some clearer sense of how education serves a public good, that individuals can succeed in college without assimilating, and that universities can shift their focuses and policies to meet the needs of a broad range of students, there will be continued challenges. Tribal colleges and universities offer some promising models for how postsecondary institutions might more effectively engage Indigenous students and Indigenous knowledge systems. By doing this, they can support tribal nations' sovereignty, self-determination, and nation-building agendas. Financially, students across the country continue to struggle with paying for college. Given the extreme poverty found in Indigenous communities and the complex financial issues tied to economic models within tribal nations, this issue will persist. A nation-building approach offers an opportunity to rethink how college is paid for and the positive contributions to be gained by completion. Finances cannot be addressed, however, without a realistic perspective of how this is influenced by poor academic preparation. This chapter and the previous one point to the need for strong K–12 preparation and the need for coordination between elementary and secondary education with tertiary education. These connections are vital to the success of students and their tribal nations. Finally, predominantly White colleges and universities may thus improve their ability to serve all students, advance equity, and facilitate social justice across various contexts.

American Indian and Alaska Native Graduate Students

WILLIAMSON (1994, P. 4) WRITES THAT "survival of the fittest" may be an extremely apropos description of the experience of Indigenous graduate students, "clearly only the strong, privileged and advantaged students survive in our higher education system," especially at the graduate level. The statistics are staggering: Of the 32,231 doctorates earned in 2009, 146 (0.04 percent) were earned by American Indian and Alaska Native students (Snyder and Dillow, 2010). Those who did "survive" share extraordinary traits (Williamson, 1994). This chapter offers a statistical portrait of AI/AN graduate students and a review of the literature describing the experiences of Indigenous students in graduate and professional programs. We conclude by exploring the extraordinary traits that have led to survival and success in higher education, as well as provide a consideration of the significance this success presents for Indigenous nation building efforts.

Research on American Indian and Alaska Native graduate education is scarce, and Indigenous student invisibility is especially pronounced at the graduate-school level (Lintner, 2003). For this chapter, we conducted a review of relevant literature over a twenty-year period, which resulted in a handful of resources: eight dissertations, two essays, and six articles, four of which were based on empirical studies. Among the eight dissertations and three research articles, eight were qualitative and three were quantitative, all contained small samples. Included are statistical data from the National Center for Education Statistics, the National Science Foundation Survey of Earned Doctorates (SED), and the Council of Graduate Schools.

A Statistical Portrait of Indigenous Graduate and Professional Students

Over the past two decades, enrollment in graduate and first-professional degrees has increased by 57 percent, from 1.7 million in 1988 to 2.7 million in 2008 (Snyder and Dillow, 2010). Total graduate enrollment, including graduate certificate, Master's programs, and doctoral programs fell 10.3 percent for American Indians/Alaskan Natives and 0.6 percent for Asians/Pacific Islanders between fall 2009 and fall 2010. This contrasts with gains of 4.5 percent for Hispanics/Latinos, 1.6 percent for Blacks/African Americans, and 0.6 percent for Whites over the same time period. Over the past decade, however, total graduate enrollment increased at a faster rate for all U.S. racial/ethnic minority groups than for Whites (Bell, 2011). Tables 10 and 11 show participation in Master's and doctoral programs by race and ethnicity. Table 12 highlights the race/ethnicity of doctoral degree recipients.

In 2009, 146 American Indian and Alaska Native students earned doctorates, representing 0.5 percent of total doctorates earned for that year. The most popular disciplines for AI/AN doctoral students were service-oriented positions, including: educational administration (13.7 percent), education research (13.7 percent), biological/biomedical sciences (13 percent), educational leadership, (9.6 percent), and psychology (8.2 percent; National Science Foundation, 2010).

TABLE 10

Percentage Distribution of Master's Degree Students' Race/Ethnicity, Selected Years

Race/Ethnicity	1995–1996	1999–2000	2003–2004	2007–2008
American Indian	0.5	0.4	0.6[a]	0.3
Asian	9.6	9.7	10.3	10.3
Black	7.5	10.0	10.5	12.9
Hispanic	4.9	6.9	8.3	8.5
White	76.2	70.6	67.8	66.1

[a]Interpret data with caution (estimates are unstable)
Source: Snyder and Dillow (2010).

TABLE 11

Percentage Distribution of Doctoral Students by Race/Ethnicity, Selected Years

Race/Ethnicity	1995–1996	1999–2000	2003–2004	2007–2008
White	69.5	65.8	61.7	62.5
Black	7.1	7.0	8.5	9.3
Hispanic	4.0	6.3	6.5	7.1
Asian/Pacific Islander	17.1	17.1	19.3	18.2
American Indian	0.4	0.5	0.7	0.3

Source: Snyder and Dillow (2010).

TABLE 12

Doctoral Degree Recipients (U.S. Citizens) by Race/Ethnicity, Selected Years 1989–2009

All Fields	1989	1994	1999	2004	2009
Total	25,062	30,904	30,317	28,038	32,231
American Indian/Alaska Native	94	143	213	131	146
Asian	1,262	3,533	2,498	2,061	2,687
Black	954	1,277	1,766	1,989	2,221
Hispanic	695	1,029	1,327	1,302	1,866
White	21,578	24,578	23,901	21,451	24,053

Source: National Science Foundation, 2010.

Indigenous students had the highest average age among doctoral recipients; averaging 38 years of age compared to 32 years for all student groups—32 years for Asian/Pacific Islander students, 37 years for Black students, 34 years for Latino/Latina students, and 32 years for White students (National Science Foundation, 2010). As shown in Table 13, AI/AN students took 9.9 years to complete doctoral degrees, ranging from 6.1 years in the physical sciences to 11.7 years in education. In most fields, doctoral degree completion for Indigenous students is longer than that of their non-Indigenous peers. Although there are many factors that influence the amount of time needed for degree completion, including access to academic, financial, and personal support, the extended amount of time for Indigenous students significantly impacts individuals,

TABLE 13

Percentage of American Indian/Alaska Native Doctoral Recipients' Primary Source of Support, 2009

All fields (number)	123.0
Teaching assistantships	8.1
Research assistantships/traineeships	13.8
Fellowships/grants	35.0
Own resources	39.0
Employer	4.1
Other	0.0

Source: National Science Foundation, 2010.

communities, and nations. The extended time to completion places heavy financial and personal pressure on the student and delays the number of graduates available to work in Indigenous communities.

The top three funding sources for Indigenous doctoral students were fellowships and grants, student's own resources, and research assistantships (National Science Foundation, 2010). The amount of education-related debt incurred by graduate students is an indicator of financial and institutional support. Indigenous doctoral recipients graduated with more debt than any other student group except for African Americans. The cumulative mean debt for African American students was $41,018 and for Native students it was $34,771. Comparatively, Latino doctoral recipients reported debt loads of $29,471, White students, $22,518, and Asian Pacific Islander students $13,294 (National Science Foundation, 2010).

Almost half (45 percent) of the AI/AN doctoral recipients for the class of 2009 reported that they had aspirations for the professoriate, 16 percent planned to work for the government, 18 percent in industry/business, 4 percent in the nonprofit sector, and 16 percent reported they would enter other fields.

The top doctoral degree institutions for Indigenous students have remained relatively steady. Table 14 shows the top twenty-two doctoral-granting institutions for Native students from 2005–2009.

TABLE 14

Top 22 Doctoral-Granting Institutions with the Largest Number of American Indian/Alaska Native Students, 2005–2009

Rank	Institution	Doctoral Recipients
	All institutions reported (193)	669
	Top 22 institutions	251
1	Oklahoma State University	30
2	Arizona State University	27
3	University of Arizona	22
4	University of North Dakota	16
6	University of Kansas	15
6	University of Minnesota	15
6	University of Oklahoma	15
8	UC Berkeley	13
9	University of Texas at Austin	11
12	Pennsylvania State University	9
12	SUNY University Buffalo	9
12	University of Michigan	9
12	University of Montana	9
12	University of Wisconsin Madison	9
18	New Mexico State University	7
18	Ohio State University	7
18	University of Arkansas	7
18	UC Davis	7
18	University of Colorado	7
18	UNC Chapel Hill	7
18	University of New Mexico	7
18	University of North Texas	7

Source: National Science Foundation, 2010.

The Experiences of Indigenous Graduate and Professional Students

Marginalization for graduate students of color is a major issue, and graduate students of color, few in number, are generally spread out across different programs of study, often having the dubious distinction of being "one of the very few," or "the only one" (Gay, 2004). Gay (2004) writes that doctoral students of color "spend their time physically isolated, and feeling excluded from the mainstream dynamics of graduate studies" (p. 267). She explains that, by comparison, White students seem to be the "favorite sons and daughters," part of the inner circle; doctoral students of color describe feeling like they are on the sidelines, watching events occur rather than participating fully in them. Given the small number of Indigenous graduate students and the even smaller number of Indigenous faculty, the feelings of isolation and alienation are especially acute for native students. The literature describing the experiences of Native doctoral students consistently describes obstacles to completing doctoral work that include feelings of isolation and academic and cultural alienation, racism and discrimination, lack of Indigenous role models, lack of academic guidance, and financial stressors. Conversely, individual resiliency and determination, supportive relationships, and cultural strengths have all been identified as sources of support that contribute to doctoral completion. Many of these obstacles are the same for Native undergraduate students, only magnified, because there are even fewer Native doctoral students and fewer role models in their communities who hold doctorates.

Feelings of Isolation and Academic and Cultural Alienation

For many students, graduate study can be an isolating endeavor. Isolation from other students, family, and community can lead to feelings of loneliness and self-doubt and, in more severe cases, to depression and dropping out (Woodford, 2005). Descriptions of isolation experienced by Native graduate students are pervasive in the literature. These feelings include feeling in exile, alone, and lonely (Buckley, 1997; Rodriguez-Rabin, 2003; Williamson, 1994), having little contact with faculty and other students in the program (Herzig, 2004), and being the only Indigenous person in the program or department (Henning, 1999; Rodriguez-Rabin, 2003; Shotton, 2008). Indigenous students also note that they are oftentimes identified as different from others—whether by skin color, by name (Ballew, 1996), by research topic (Ballew, 1996; Henning, 1999), or by worldview (Williamson, 1994)—creating intense feelings of isolation that take emotional and intellectual energy better directed toward academic pursuits. Emotional stress from isolation may affect cognitive activities such as concentration, focus, judgment, memory, attention to detail, and error frequency (Fisher, 1994, as cited in Gay, 2004).

Academic and cultural alienation refers to the balancing act where students feel they have to "manage" their cultural integrity as an Indigenous person in ways that conform to the norms of graduate school. For many, learning how to navigate the system means not being free to act wholly like one's own self. In her ethnographic study, Buckley (1997) explored the university experiences of AI/AN graduate and professional students and found that students experienced academic alienation as a result of having too few colleagues who share their culture. Academic alienation is compounded when other students, and especially faculty, are unfamiliar with Indigenous perspectives and therefore unable to understand and/or help students develop ideas.

Even unofficial university/departmental practices may make students feel out of place. Students experience constant conflict between what is expected of them as tribal members and what is expected of them in the academy. By being responsible to their tribe, students risk being a disappointment to the academy. One of the women in Shotton's study described preparing for her dissertation defense:

> there was a policy, you can't do [catered meals], just cookies and coffee and stuff like that. And I thought, "I wonder what I can bring?". . . it was [a] big deal at [the university], I was getting my Ph.D. as a Native student . . . so they [the Native community on campus] wanted to have this feast for me at their longhouse. It was fry bread and stew and bread pudding, an all Native meal . . . this event is kind of unfolding and I have no control over it . . . and it was kind of scary to me that I was breaking with this cookies and coffee, and I was doing it at the longhouse, because you typically do it in the Dean's office in the college . . . this would have been the first defense in this newly built longhouse . . . I was like "Holy shit!" . . . I was very excited, but also very self-conscious . . . you know, my professors are going to frown on this [Shotton, 2008, p. 180].

Although we know that engagement in academic and preprofessional programs is important to academic success (Herzig, 2004), commitment to community may make it difficult for some Native students to participate in research-related and extracurricular academic activities and events, further isolating students from the communities of their department, especially in programs that are inflexible and built around narrow models of how students should participate in departmental communities. On the other hand, studying in graduate programs far from home means Indigenous students may not have access to their primary sources of support—family and community (Heionen, 2002; Moon, 2003; Secatero, 2009).

Like Native undergraduate students, Native graduate students who are geographically isolated from their communities may not be able to go home and participate in familial, religious, and tribal events, especially those that occur in the middle of a semester (Heionen, 2002). In addition, pressure to conform to the academy may lead to students feeling like they have to distance themselves from family and culture and, therefore, like they are forced to reconcile living in "two worlds" (Ballew, 1996). Many American Indian graduate students, many of whom are the first in their family to go to college, feel they cannot discuss their graduate school experiences or seek advice from family members (Shotton, 2008; Rodriguez-Rabin, 2003). Rodriguez-Rabin (2003) describes the personal costs of going to graduate school as being caught between her people and her ambitions. She wrote:

> *Once a person of color leaves his/her hometown, they cannot go back. Your family looks at you differently. I cannot even change the oil in my truck without being told to go sit down and do what I normally do; read. With awkward looks and mixed emotions, I go to the truck seat that sits on the oil stained concrete and I try to read [p. 394].*

Family members may not have firsthand understanding of the struggles facing Indigenous graduate students and the intense pressure for them to assimilate, yet they are reported as providing the most support for graduate school. Parents and extended family who did not have opportunities to go to college may not be able to provide typical forms of support such as financial assistance, guidance for coursework, or suggestions for summer internships leading to professional positions postgraduation. Indigenous families do possess a rich array of cultural wealth. Cultural wealth can be defined as "the array of knowledge, skills, abilities and contacts possessed and utilized by communities of color to survive and resist macro and micro forms of oppression" (Yosso, 2005, p. 77). Cultural wealth is a critical race theory challenge to traditional interpretations of cultural capital and shifts the lens from a deficit view of communities of color, instead focusing on sources of strength and resiliency (Perez-Huber, 2009; Villalpando and Solórzano, 2005; Yosso, 2005). Villalpando and Solórzano (2005) argue that traditional notions of Bourdieuian cultural capital are based on social class and should be reconceptualized by taking into consideration the cultural wealth of students of color, their families, and their communities. In this instance, cultural wealth includes values and applications of those values through practice of Indigenous families and tribal communities that support student enrollment and success in graduate school, and that would not be considered forms of cultural capital within a traditional Bourdieuian framework.

Yosso (2005, p. 79) extends cultural-wealth theory by describing six unique forms of cultural wealth, including *familial capital*, which "refers to those cultural knowledges nurtured among *familial* (kin) that carry a sense of community history, memory, and cultural intuition . . . This form of cultural wealth engages a commitment to community well-being and expands the concept of family to include a more broad understanding of kinship. . . ." Research on AI/AN graduate students reveals that Indigenous families provide support by offering words of encouragement and prayers, for example, "My mom would be back at her place on the rez and she'd be doing prayers for me . . . My sisters were doing it for me now . . . if something is going on, I just say, 'Burn some cedar for me'" (Shotton, 2008, p. 145). Additionally, there are some interesting examples of the connections between families, communities, and spiritual life. One individual notes:

At the beginning of each school year I'd return to the home of my grandparents to receive protection prayers. Before I left for the Ivy League, I took part in the Beauty Way Ceremony. Prior to sending off any important scholarship and school applications, I always returned home to make offerings with my grandfather. We made

offerings to ask for assistance and each time I was supported
[Secatero, 2009, p. 141].

Other examples of Indigenous familial capital include providing for basic necessities such as meals, housing, and child care, attending a dissertation defense (Shotton, 2008), receiving letters from family members (Secatero, 2009), or attending students' presentations at conferences.

Racism and Discrimination

The literature describes both blatant and covert racism directed at Indigenous graduate and professional students. Examples of this included Native students being expected to speak on behalf of all American Indians, feeling that they had to work twice as hard to prove they were capable and belonged in the academy, and feeling tokenized in their programs (Moon, 2003; Shotton, 2008). Shotton's study of American Indian women doctoral recipients from federally recognized tribes found that students felt as if they had to perform at a higher level of academic standard than their peers. A perennial stereotype that students of color worry about is whether other graduate students and faculty will have low expectations of them (Woodford, 2005); they thus experience additional anxiety because they feel that they have to work harder than other students to prove themselves. Many American Indian and Alaska Native graduate students share the feelings of this woman:

> *. . .if we try to be super people then we're hurting ourselves, because the person next to me in class is not trying to be super person and that person is getting their degree done, getting their dissertation done, getting their degree, getting a job and I'm still over here writing my dissertation because of those expectations [Shotton, 2008, p. 144].*

This student explains the double bind students often find themselves in: Either expectations of them are so low that Native students feel they must prove they belong in the university, or, because Native students may be a part of a small minority of students on campus, they believe that even higher expectations are placed upon them. Thus they begin to feel they need to be a "super graduate student." This perception of having to be super may lead to stifling feelings of trying to be perfect or to do well because the resulting success may influence faculty perceptions not only of the individual but of Indigenous peoples as a whole. Having unattainable expectations placed upon oneself can cause paralysis if one is not able to perform as expected.

Several authors described how Native students experienced being silenced in their programs, resulting in withdrawal from classroom discussions and other interactions with faculty and peers (Ballew, 1996; Buckley, 1997; Henning, 1999; Lacourt, 2003; Rodriguez-Rabin, 2003; Shotton, 2008). The act of silencing students is blatantly racist and at times aggressive. Some Indigenous students explain that it was a combination of treatment in the classroom as well as cultural socialization that made it incredibly difficult, and at times painful, for them to speak out in class, articulate opposing points of view, and question cherished theories and academic assumptions. Lacourt (2003, pp. 288–289) described an experience where she had a different interpretation of theory used in class and spoke up for the first time in that course; the response was absolute silence from the students and professor. She explains, "I felt like there was no place for my ideas, my questions, and my understandings in this course. I felt humiliated and stupid—as if somehow my comments were not sophisticated enough or academically sound." She writes about the tensions between being silenced in the classroom by students and faculty and yet remembering her father saying "don't speak until you are spoken to or have something to say." Being successful in her graduate program felt uncomfortable because it meant having to act assertively and adopt the vocabulary and concepts of non-Indian educators and bureaucrats and follow along in lockstep.

The feeling of being silenced extended beyond the classroom. Henning (1999) wrote that some Native students felt uncomfortable sharing aspects of their lives because cultural differences might be taken up, interpreted, and stereotyped by faculty and peers.

Indigenous graduate students face stereotypes of themselves, their families, and their communities. Ballew (1996) writes that stereotypes result in false assumptions, insensitive ignorance, and blatant racist comments by faculty and students. Shotton (2008, p. 135) describes the experience of one of the women in her study who shared a draft of her dissertation with her chair. The student's chair was surprised that the student used pseudonyms that were not stereotypically American Indian: "'I thought you were going to call her White Feather or Babbling Brook.' I don't know what bullshit names she was using, but she thought that my pseudonyms were going to be Indian maiden names. And that's how awful she was! And she's my major professor. . . ."

American Indian and Alaska Native graduate and professional students are deliberate and sometimes cautious about how they respond to these kinds of interactions. The women doctoral students in Shotton's (2008) study were portrayed as combative in their programs if they expressed divergent opinions or asked questions—both of which were indicative of challenging the academic status quo. In order to be successful, the women had to find ways to adapt, to balance how to express their viewpoints without being viewed as angry and combative. They felt pressure to be unobtrusive and to temper their responses so as not to make their White classmates and faculty uncomfortable.

Constant exposure to racial microaggressions produce emotional, psychological, and physiological distress resulting in "racial battle fatigue" (Smith, Hung, and Franklin, 2011). Smith, Yosso, and Solórzano (2011) use a critical race framework to adapt Pierce's (1995) work on microaggressions in order to address how students of color experience microaggressions in the academy. They define microaggressions as:

1) subtle verbal and nonverbal insults directed at people of color, often automatically and unconsciously; 2) layered insults, based on one's race, gender, class, sexuality, language, immigration status, phenotype, accent, or surname; and 3) cumulative insults, which cause unnecessary stress to people of color while privileging whites [p. 845].

Students of color experience constant microaggressions, resulting in what has been termed mundane, extreme, environmental stress (MEES; Smith, Hung, and Franklin, 2011), leading to mental, emotional, physical, and academic strain and, ultimately, racial battle fatigue. Smith, Hung, and Franklin (2011) posit that one of the consequences of educational attainment is that students of color are exposed to increased MEES in historically White institutions

(HWIs). Native graduate students then, by virtue of their educational achievement, are at greater risk of racial battle fatigue because of prolonged exposure to incessant microagressions.

Lack of Indigenous Role Models

All graduate and professional students benefit from role models they admire and whose lives they want to emulate. At HWIs, it is challenging for students of color to find role models based on shared outlook and connections to similar experiences. Students of color describe wanting to find role models who "look like me," "someone who immediately understands my experiences and perspectives," or "someone whose very presence lets me know I, too, can make it to the academy" (Woodford, 2005). Native graduate students look for affinity with role models who have paved the way, who have worked through dissonances between their home communities and the academic community, and who can help students do the same (Kidwell, 1986).

It is a gross understatement to say there is a need for more Native faculty throughout the academic pipeline (Ballew, 1996; Kidwell, 1986; Moon, 2003; Williamson, 1994). Native students at the undergraduate level see few Indigenous graduate students and even fewer Indigenous faculty (Kidwell, 1986). Along with the lack of role models, there is an absence of pictures, paintings, statues, and other symbols that indicate that colleges and universities embrace the lives and histories of Indigenous people and tribal nations (Henning, 1999). Overall, then, we might ask how academic life is modeled for American Indian and Alaska Native doctoral students. For some, the absence of this modeling results in little hope that they can have balanced lives where they can achieve success in the professoriate, nurture their own families, and at the same time continue to serve their own and other Indigenous communities.

Lack of Academic Guidance

This absence of modeling starts early and means that AI/AN students often miss out on effective advising and counseling regarding the pursuit of graduate education (Heionen, 2002). As we have argued above, not having experience with the system and the rules of higher education places Indigenous students at a significant disadvantage (Ballew, 1996), which in turn hurts Native families and tribal nations.

Patterson, Baldwin, and Olsen (2009) analyzed admission data from 107 American Indian and Alaska Native medical school applicants employing a numerical and open-ended survey to explore the supports and obstacles for the medical school application process. Just over a third of the thirty-four respondents (35 percent) indicated that they had received incorrect information or discouraging advice from counselors and faculty when applying. Students who were not encouraged early on their undergraduate careers to pursue medicine indicated that they became interested in becoming a doctor too late to prepare well and take courses that would prepare them for the MCAT. Lack of information about the application process and about medical school was the by-product of factors that included a lack of formal university-based counseling and support coupled with the fact that many students were the first one on their family to apply to medical school. One student who had been rejected for medical school shared this response: "No guidance. No one knows what an Indian needs to do to get into medical school, only the schools themselves, and they rarely are in a position to advise . . . We don't have the benefit of having a father or a relative who is a doctor and can advise us" (Patterson, Baldwin, and Olsen, 2009, p. 316).

In addition to missing academic guidance, some Indigenous students are told outright "you can't do it," and are discouraged from pursuing graduate work (Lacourt, 2003; Patterson, Baldwin, and Olsen, 2009). Others are told that they simply do not qualify (Williamson, 1994) and are similarly discouraged from even applying to graduate and professional programs. Like other underrepresented students, Indigenous students, especially those with fellowships, may be overlooked for teaching and research assistantships and as a result, they experience fewer opportunities for career-building interactions with faculty and miss out on other professional opportunities that can enhance their curriculum vitae (Woodford, 2005).

Financial Stressors

In the study by Patterson, Baldwin, and Olsen (2009), half of the survey respondents indicated that money was the cause of several problems; for example, courses designed to prepare students for the LSAT, GRE, and MCAT are pricey, or students may be unable to take time off to study for the exam. Several students also indicated that the expense of submitting admission applications coupled with the prohibitive costs to travel to campuses for interviews limited the range of institutions where they could apply for medical school. Limb's (2001) study of American Indian students in professional social work programs found that, compared to other student groups, Native students in his study were more likely to be caring for children or other family members. Heionen (2002) also found that lack of adequate funding also meant having to wait to buy books and supplies, compromising academic success or making it that much harder to compete.

Collectively, emotional and intellectual stress caused by feelings of isolation, academic and cultural alienation, racism and discrimination, and financial stressors place an extra, burdensome tax on Indigenous graduate students. Hanna (2005) writes that Indigenous doctoral students do not adapt passively to their environments; they respond in diverse ways to refashion environments to meet their individual needs and their desire to serve their community.

Sources of Support

Research on graduate students of color points to the resiliency and self-motivation of these individuals. There are a number of factors that support persistence and success for Indigenous graduate students; these include individual determination and resiliency, supportive relationships, including mentoring, and the desire to give back to one's tribe and support Native communities. Several studies revealed that successful Native doctoral students described themselves as "persistent," "tenacious," "determined" and "goal committed" (Moon, 2003; Henning, 1999; Neuerbug, 2000; Secatero, 2009; Shotton, 2008). The women in Shotton's study shared that a love of learning and a passion for research gave them the motivation to complete their programs and that much of their tenaciousness had been developed surviving the academy as an undergraduate. Secatero (2009) found that spiritual, mental, social, and physical well-being were individual characteristics that contributed to students' resiliency and success.

Universally, access to Indigenous faculty was noted as an important source of support, and in many cases, students described having to go outside of their department to find mentors who in some cases were other faculty of color (Shotton, 2008). In several studies, consistent with research on Indigenous undergraduate students (Shotton, Oosahwe, and Cintrón, 2007), Indigenous graduate students responded to isolation and cultural discontinuity by creating a surrogate community comprised of Native students on campus (Williamson, 1994). Students were either able to join existing campus groups, such as the Native American Student Association (Neuerbug, 2000), or they created communities by themselves. A student in Hanna's study (2005) shared:

> A group of female, Native, graduate students met once a week for a brown bag lunch, no pun intended, to talk about any issues, concerns any of us might have. This group was truly a lifesaver for me . . . participation in this group gave me hope that I could complete my program. I perceived these women as being similar to me, so I felt that I could achieve what they achieved [p. 94].

In some cases students created communities of support with Native students at other institutions by attending conferences; in other cases doctoral students were able to develop supportive networks with other Native doctoral students and faculty through participation in professional organizations such as the National Affairs Administrators in Higher Education (NASPA) or the National Congress of American Indians (NCAI).

Finally, students' desires to give back to their tribal communities and to Indigenous communities broadly were noted as significant motivators for completing doctoral programs (Moon, 2003; Henning, 1999; Lacourt, 2003; Neuerbug, 2000; Secatero, 2009; Shotton, 2008).

Contrary to notions of success as the attainment of wealth, eminence, or favor, success for many Indigenous students is located in contributing to their tribe and family. Native students typically talk about the importance of earning a degree in terms of what it will enable them to do for their communities (Brayboy, 2006; Shotton, 2008).

Graduate Education and Nation Building

The lens of Indigenous nation building provides context for better understanding American Indian and Alaska Native student participation in graduate and professional school; it also forces a strong critique of the current system that is clearly not meeting the needs of Indigenous students, Native communities, and tribal nations. As we have noted throughout this monograph, strong, healthy nations require Indigenous individuals who have been educationally successful. The success experienced by the relatively small number of AI/AN graduate and professional students and alumni highlights the importance of the knowledge and skill sets these degrees present for Indigenous communities. Graduate and professional school participation is not simply about adding letters behind one's name; it is about being positioned to serve one's community in ways that may not be possible without having attained that success. We need look no further than the American Indian and Alaska Native PhDs, MDs, and JDs that we know—these individuals mentor other Indigenous students at all points along the pipeline, they create and direct programs that meet countless community needs for culturally responsive teachers and other professionals, they advocate and shape policies and practices that are in the best interest of Native communities, and the list goes on.

As we have seen throughout this chapter, Indigenous students face great odds, most acutely in graduate degree programs. They often come from families in which neither parent has a college degree; they have a harder time accessing financial, academic, and personal support mechanisms to finish their degree, and those who do finish often take longer than students from any other race/ethnicity. Still, those who make it through do so because they tend to be driven by a strong desire to serve their communities. This is evident in the most popular disciplines for American Indian/Alaska Native doctoral students. Interest in fields such as educational administration, research, and leadership as well as biological/biomedical sciences and psychology suggests students are interested in particular types of education, training, knowledge, and skill sets. Pursuing careers in these fields likely allows Indigenous students to give back to the community in ways the community needs most. Whether by revamping educational policies and curriculum so that it better reflects and validates community knowledge and practices, or by becoming psychologists out of a desire to change the field of therapy so it better reflects the needs of Indigenous communities and is better able to address complex issues Indigenous communities are facing—these statistics are a very telling portrait of student desires that may easily fold into a tribal nation-building agenda.

American Indian and Alaska Native Faculty

THROUGHOUT THIS MONOGRAPH, we have made links between higher education and tribal nation building. We've argued that in order for tribal nations to be economically and politically successful, they must also be educationally successful. Pursuing higher education is part of the larger nation-building agenda, and the pursuit of knowledge through colleges and universities is critical for the development and maintenance of strong, healthy, and sustainable Indigenous communities. These connections between higher education and nation building are especially apparent when we consider the presence (or lack thereof) of Indigenous faculty in U.S. colleges and universities. Indigenous faculty play such a central role in the process of higher education toward nation building that we must understand what it means to be an Indigenous faculty member in mainstream institutions, as well as think deeply about policies and practices that will facilitate increased participation by American Indian and Alaska Native scholars in colleges and universities. Table 15 offers a snapshot of full-time faculty in institutions based on race/ethnicity.

Currently, there are few American Indian and Alaska Native faculty in mainstream colleges and universities, making such faculty one of the smallest segments of American higher education (Cross, 1991; Turner, Gonzalez, and Wood, 2011). American Indian and Alaska Natives represent 5 percent of U.S. faculty compared to 79 percent White, 6 percent Asian Pacific Islander, 7 percent Black, and 4 percent Latino (Almanac of Higher Education, 2011). Nationally, Indigenous faculty make up roughly 0.5 percent of the faculty in four-year-degree–granting institutions, and 0.7 percent of the faculty in

TABLE 15

Full-Time Faculty in Degree-Granting Institutions, Fall 2009

Academic rank	White	Black	Latino	APA	AI/AN	Nonresident alien
Professor	85.1	3.5	2.7	7.6	0.3	0.8
Associate professor	80.0	5.6	3.7	8.6	0.4	1.7
Assistant professor	70.6	6.6	4.1	11.2	0.4	7.1
Instructors	77.5	7.7	6.5	5.5	1.0	1.8
Lecturers	76.7	5.6	4.9	7.1	0.4	5.3
Other faculty	70.3	5.4	3.4	8.0	8.0	12.5

Source: Almanac of Higher Education (2011).

public two-year institutions, whereas White faculty make up roughly 80 percent or more of the faculty across institutional types.

Of the 3,457 total American Indian and Alaska Native faculty members in Fall 2009, a slight majority taught in the field of education, comprising 2.2 percent of education faculty, followed by the humanities (1.8 percent), health and business (1.6 percent each), and social sciences and fine art (1.4 percent each; Snyder and Dillow, 2010). There are nearly equal numbers of Native male (1,737) and female faculty (1,720), although male faculty are more likely to hold the rank of Professor or Associate Professor than females. Indigenous faculty are more concentrated in states with a large proportion of American Indians, such as Arizona and Oklahoma (Pavel and others, 1998; Fox, 2008).

Indigenous faculty are frequently not included in national studies and data-gathering efforts, and there are only a handful of empirical studies on or that include Native faculty. The dearth of information limits our ability to understand and resolve the issues these faculty encounter in higher education (Tippeconnic and McKinney, 2003). In this chapter, research literature on Indigenous faculty is reviewed, along with more than a dozen essay articles and chapters written by Native faculty describing their experiences in mainstream academic institutions. Prominent throughout the literature are several common themes. These include the role of Native faculty as activists, advocates and change agents in higher education; their role in Native nation building and their service to tribal communities; and a number of persistent institutional barriers and burdens that marginalize Native faculty and block their advancement in tenure and promotion.

Transforming the Academy as Activists and Advocates

Native faculty serve as activists, advocates, and change agents in postsecondary institutions and in their disciplines by challenging dominant, racist, and discriminatory scholarship, practices and perceptions; by stimulating research in Indigenous issues; by developing and infusing curriculum that is inclusive of Native perspectives and scholarship; by assisting colleges and universities in recruiting and retaining Native students; and through networking with Native organizations. These organizations include the National Indian Education Association, the American Indian Higher Education Association, American Education Research Association Indigenous Peoples of the Americas special interest group, The Native American Rights Fund, The National Congress of American Indians, The National Indian Policy Commission, The Association of American Indian and Alaska Native Professors, and tribal governments and communities.

There is little understanding among higher education leaders, faculty, and staff about the history, culture, legal status, values, and goals of tribal nations (Champagne, 2007). The research and scholarly contributions of Native faculty in fields such as education, medicine, public health, archeology, anthropology, psychology, political science, law, history, linguistics, and the humanities are changing disciplinary paradigms by the creation of new theoretical, methodological, and practical applications infused with the writings, voices, and knowledge of Indigenous people (Atalay, 2006; de la Torre, 2004; Champagne, 2004; Deloria, 2004; Dana-Sacco, 2010; James, 2004; Kidwell, 2009; Hunter; 2004; Nicholas, 2006; Two Bears, 2006; Smith and Jackson, 2006; McCallum, 2009; Tippeconnic and McKinney, 2003).

By way of example, Hunter (2004) writes that she feels responsible as a Native faculty in an archeology department to teach about federal and state repatriation laws and how to improve research ethics and practice in archeology by respecting Indigenous perspectives in cultural heritage preservation and management. An example of change at the institutional level includes the Native American Studies program at the University of Nebraska–Omaha, where guiding principles include cultural recovery in the service of Nebraska's urban

Indian population. Deloria (2004) notes that standard courses in archaeology and anthropology that had been traditionally offered as "Indian" courses have been replaced with courses dealing with federal Indian policy and contemporary affairs that are much more directly relevant to the needs of Native nations.

Native faculty also serve a critical role in mentoring and advising students. Not only do they advise students within their departments and disciplinary areas, Indigenous faculty typically mentor Indigenous students from across campus and advise other students of color and White students interested in Native issues (Deloria, 2004; Turner and Myers, 2000; Stein, 1996). This is consistent with other research showing that racially diverse faculty assist in the recruitment and retention of students of color in higher education (Antonio, 2000; Turner, Gonzalez, and Wood, 2011). In a national study of faculty, Umbach (2011) found that American Indian faculty more frequently interact with students than White faculty, even after controlling for disciplinary differences and institutional type. He found that faculty of color, including American Indian faculty, employed active and collaborative techniques more frequently than their White faculty peers, and made significant contributions to student learning and involvement by creating environments that fostered diverse interactions.

Indigenous Faculty and Nation Building

Native scholars typically orient their work so that it benefits Native communities and tribal nations (Cross; 1991; Dana-Sacco, 2010; Faircloth, 2009; Fox, 2008; Stein, 1996; Tippeconnic and McKinney, 2003). In so doing, Native faculty are instrumental in the educational and economic advancement of tribal communities (Cross, 1991) and in helping to preserve, record, and recover Indigenous forms of knowledge (Wilson, 2004). Kidwell (2009, p. 11) argues that the challenge is to link the intellectual work of the academy to the real-life needs of tribal nations, where community members "do not have the luxury of knowing what a research agenda is, let alone formulating one."

Although Native faculty play important roles in Native nation-building efforts and have made significant inroads transforming a variety of aspects of higher education, there remain "extraordinary roadblocks in their path toward academic parity. Although there continues to be a demand for Indian professors, opportunities continue to be restricted to entry-level positions, and within the university Indian professors are marginalized by traditional academic expectations" (Deloria, 2004, pp. 17–18).

Native Faculty at Mainstream Institutions

In her research on American Indian women faculty, Fox (2008) found that participants expressed joy and satisfaction in being able to pursue their intellectual passions, in having academic freedom and autonomy, and in having the flexibility to do research and writing. The faculty in her study also shared feeling tremendously rewarded by teaching, mentoring, and contributing to their respective fields, especially prizing their roles in giving back to their home communities and tribal nations. Similarly, Susan Faircloth, Director of the American Indian Education Leadership Program at Pennsylvania State University writes, "Fortunately, I have been blessed with a job that allows me the flexibility to work wherever I may be rather than being place bound. This means that my work can and does travel with me wherever I go. The challenge is being careful not to be overwhelmed by the intensity of or passion for this work" (Faircloth, forthcoming, p. 9).

Notwithstanding the positive aspects of faculty life and the ability to serve Native communities through academic pursuits, several themes emerged in the literature describing barriers to Native faculty advancement. These themes paralleled the experiences described by Native graduate students, including 1) feelings of isolation and a lack of encouragement for their research interests, 2) lack of mentorship and institutional support, 3) cultural discontinuity, and 4) racism and discrimination.

Isolation and Lack of Encouragement for Research Interests
Similar to Indigenous graduate students, American Indian and Alaska Native faculty are such a rarity in mainstream colleges and universities that they frequently describe feeling isolated and lonely. They often have to look outside of their departments or institutions for a community of scholars to share their work (Fox, 2008; Peterson-Hickey, 1998). Research by Jayakumar, Howard,

and Allen (2009) on racial privilege and campus climate as experienced by faculty of color found that individual background characteristics seem to have a small effect on retention, whereas the quality of experiences once the individual arrives at the institution have the greatest impact on retention. Even tenure did not completely eliminate the negative effects of a hostile racial climate. They also found that faculty who perceived that their work was valued by the department were more likely to be retained in the professoriate. In disaggregating faculty of color, they found that American Indian (44 percent) faculty more often reported an intention to leave the academy, followed by African American (39 percent), Latino/Latina (36 percent), and Asian American faculty (27 percent). Native faculty also report lack of support for their research efforts, a devaluing of the journals where they publish, and feeling like they have to work harder to earn respect as scholars (Fox, 2008; Calhoun, 2003; Deloria, 2004; Innes, 2009; Stein, 1996).

A major concern among Indigenous faculty is the difficulty in maintaining ties with their own tribal community while at the same time being part of an academic community (Turner and Meyers, 2000). As a result of their ties to tribal communities, Indigenous faculty often provide assistance or service to meet tribal needs, taking the risk that their service might not be valued or recognized within their institutions, and thus jeopardizing how they may be perceived in the promotion and tenure process (Turner and Myers, 2000; Tippeconnic and McKinney, 2003). Wilson (2004) writes:

> *Since the recovery of other forms of knowledge requires abandoning or challenging existing academic norms, many Indigenous scholars have chosen to protect their institutional status rather than risk being denied tenure and promotion because their research and publication was not "scholarly enough." Fortunately, there seems to be a growing number of us who are less concerned about our status in the white world and more concerned with helping our respective nations with long-term survival, and who also realize the value of our traditional ways of knowing . . . While many of us organize our research agendas based on directives from our communities, the academy often resists responsiveness to those directives [p. 77].*

As a Native scholar, Calhoun (2003) describes her work as a social obligation to her community. She argues that postsecondary institutions ask Indigenous scholars to pay a high price for membership that includes silencing their own voices and those of their community, resulting in a loss to personal autonomy and to the sovereignty of tribal nations. She adds that such practices contradict academic freedom and the creation of new knowledge. Deloria (2004) writes that Native scholars are judged by wholly inappropriate criteria, which requires them to publish in prestigious journals even though the gatekeepers of these journals keep them closed to anyone outside the journal "in" group. Moreover, it is well documented that faculty of color are more likely to pursue research related to issues of race and ethnicity, gender, equity, and social justice (Turner and Meyers, 1999; Jayakumar, Howard, and Allen, 2009), issues that may be perceived as overly political and, therefore, not scholarly within the academic community. Furthermore, White faculty have the privilege of being defined and evaluated as individuals, whereas faculty of color often experience pressure of knowing that their victories and their failures will be taken to represent an entire racial/ethnic group (Jayakumar, Howard, and Allen, 2009).

Lack of Mentorship and Institutional Support

James (2004, p. 48) writes that, "Natives in academe often seem to find themselves excluded from access to important information, excluded from important decisions, and excluded from important resources." This has also been described as witnessing White colleagues receive a seemingly different level of mentorship and "looking after" by senior faculty. Mentoring is a crucial strategy for success, and Fox (2008) found that although mentors do not have to be American Indian or Alaska Native, it makes a substantial and positive difference when Indigenous faculty are available. Mentoring is crucial for sharing with junior faculty the hidden rules and unarticulated departmental and institutional expectations required for advancement.

Deloria (2004, p. 29) laments that Indigenous scholars have not had the benefit of informal academic networks and as a result, are "failing to gain tenure and promotion because they have no connection to influential white scholars who can be mustered to plead their case. . . . Indian scholars must spend considerably more time planning their academic futures, developing allies within academic circles, and cultivating contacts outside the institutional setting in which they find themselves." Breinig (2003), an Alaska Native faculty, describes that in the absence of other Alaska Native faculty or other mentors at her university she wishes she would have known earlier to connect with scholars engaged in similar work by attending the American Indian and Alaska Native Professors conference. She shared that a presentation from senior scholars helped her find ways to situate her own tribal work in academia.

Replete in the literature by and about Indigenous faculty issues is lack of institutional support and being saddled with institutional burdens in ways that White faculty are not. Native faculty spend an inordinate amount of time and effort serving on committees and advising Indigenous students who may not even be in the classes they teach or on their student-advising roles (Cross, 1991; Fox, 2008; Hunt and Harrington, 2008; Peterson-Hickey, 1998; Stein, 1996). Although advising and mentoring students can be extremely rewarding, it can also be time consuming, especially when non-Native faculty and administrators refer Native students to Indigenous faculty in their stead. In addition to being a kind of "shadow work" (Fassinger, 2008) that is not taken into consideration for promotion and tenure, there is a danger that the administration may begin to hold Indigenous faculty somehow accountable for the success of Indigenous students, relieving other non-Indigenous faculty and staff of their responsibilities toward Native students (Stein, 1996; Hunt and Harrington, 2008).

There are so few Indigenous faculty on campuses that university committees vigorously compete for their time and service, which takes time away from their research and writing (Cross, 1991; Deloria, 2004; Fox, 2008; Kidwell, 1990; Peterson-Hickey, 1998; Stein, 1996). Tierney and Bensimon (1996) use the term "cultural taxation" to refer to burdens placed on faculty of color to meet expectations for institutional and community service. Native faculty are perpetually expected to represent all Indigenous people in formal and informal interactions, and to have expertise related to Indigenous people in all areas (Fox, 2008; Kidwell, 1990). Deloria (2004) outlines, very honestly and very specifically, the unbalanced responsibilities AI/AN faculty are saddled with in comparison to their White counterparts. He argues that an absolute requirement in protecting minority scholars would be to make clear the radical differences between the demands placed on racialized scholars and those placed on White scholars. He wryly observes that:

> *The Indian professor will always be on a variety of committees so the university can claim that Indians were consulted and represented in whatever harebrained scheme the administrators have conceived. Since the Indian professors will be junior they will probably have to serve on departmental committees, and if there is a protest about anything affecting Indians and the university they will be expected to support the university without question. The Indian professor's day will be disrupted countless times as he or she will be regarded as an authority on anything remotely dealing with Indians. And university fundraisers will pester the Indian scholar whenever there is a chance for the university to get grants. They will expect scholars to enthusiastically endorse proposals even though they know that the majority of people who will be hired will be non-Indians [p. 28].*

Deloria continues that for Native scholars, community service is an almost overwhelming burden because Native faculty must continually prove to both university personnel and other Indians that they are an active part of the local community. Indigenous faculty are constantly confronted with expectations of public service that include conducting research for tribal communities or governments, representing the community at meetings, or serving as tribal council members or nonprofit board members (Cross, 1991). Although scholars of color find solace in safe spaces such as their family, community, and church, the commitment to community that is honored by many American Indian/Alaska Native, African American, and Latino faculty, in particular, can be a constant source of frustration when it competes with the kind of productivity that counts for tenure and promotion (Stanley, 2011). In describing her own efforts to find a balance between her work as a professor, service to community, and her role as a daughter, sister, aunt, wife, and mother, Faircloth's (forthcoming) sentiment reflects the experiences of many Indigenous faculty:

Over the years, I've come to terms with the fact that a large part of giving back and making a difference involves engaging in service-related activities. This means sometimes making a conscious decision to engage in service when the academy tells me to write or taking time to talk with parents and families about their rights in the special education process when the academy tells me I should be using this time to collect data. In the end, I attempt to do it all. I engage in service, I collect data, and I write. I meet the expectations of the academy, but foremost, I strive to do so in ways that are honoring to Indigenous peoples and communities [p. 4].

Cultural Discontinuity

The values of Native people are often in direct conflict with the careerist attitudes and ambitions of the professoriate. "The academic role is somewhat of an egotistical exercise; competing and being a star are not necessarily the appropriate things to do for Indian people" (Peterson-Hickey, 1998, p. 161). Faircloth (forthcoming) uses the term "academic self-centeredness" to refer to time she felt she needed to spend focusing on writing the year prior to tenure. And Cross (1991) explains that the pressure to excel as an individual is opposite of what is expected of Native people as community members, and that being at the center of attention, which is important to receiving recognition in the department, is uncomfortable for some Native faculty.

Racism and Discrimination

Similar to the experiences of Native graduate students, Indigenous faculty describe experiencing overt and covert racism and discrimination. Examples of more overt racism include direct confrontations through comments or actions by other faculty and staff who did not recognize the Native scholar as a faculty member. In the following story, an Indigenous male faculty describes getting to campus early and reading the paper in his car. He parked in a lot near the edge of the campus to be in the shade but was accosted by three campus security guards who demanded to know why he was on campus. He was told that a faculty member had seen him park and was uncomfortable that he was loitering in that parking area without a parking sticker, despite the fact that he was in a lot that did not require a parking sticker. The faculty who complained also noted he was in an "older car." He was questioned and detained by campus security until one of the guards was able to contact someone in his department to verify that he was a faculty member (White, 2003).

Less overt forms of racism include the constant tokenizing of Indigenous faculty that comes with the expectation for Native faculty to play the role of the Indian expert, to speak for all Indigenous people, and the command performance of Native faculty on university and departmental committees dealing with race/ethnicity (Fox, 2008; Peterson-Hickey, 1998; Stanley, 2011; Stein, 1996). Deloria (2004, p. 20) comments how unfortunate it is that part of the legacy retired and emeritus Native faculty have left for the current generation of Indian scholars is regenerated racism. "One need only glance at the intellectual landscape in higher education to understand how deep the effects of race are. In the advanced degree programs in every college and university there is an engrained belief that Indians are not only inferior but also that they know virtually nothing about their communities." According to Deloria, there is an almost automatic acceptance of anti-Indian themes in academia. White scholars will not, as a rule, defend attacks against the scholarship of their Indigenous colleagues because of racist assumptions about the quality and relevance of their work. The assumption often remains that AI/AN faculty are only offered faculty positions as affirmative action hires, implying that they could not otherwise qualify for the positions (Deloria, 2004).

Indigenous Faculty in Tribal Colleges and Universities

Indigenous faculty experiences in tribal colleges and universities are in many ways very different than they are in nontribal institutions. The cultural identities of TCUs affect virtually every aspect of college life, and it is in this context that TCU faculty work. Tribal college and university curricula play a crucial role in the struggle for tribal sovereignty and self-determination, and the faculty charge is to integrate tribal culture into the curricula and pedagogical practices (Bad Wound, 1991; Tippeconnic and McKinney, 2003). Tribal college faculty strive to make their courses more culturally relevant by modifying teaching methods, and by recognizing that Indigenous students typically prefer cooperation over competition (Boyer, 2005). For example, a math teacher might encourage group work or allow students to raise their scores by retaking an exam, reflecting, in part, a tribally based value of forgiveness (Boyer, 2005). Bad Wound (1991, p. 15) states that TCUs, "should respond to personal needs, from the simple to the profound, not simply by 'giving students a break,' but by having ways to recognize why a student is having trouble and having the flexibility to respond in culturally appropriate ways."

According to AIHEC (2007) American Indians and Alaska Natives comprise 64 percent of the faculty, administrators, and staff at tribal colleges and universities. The number of Indigenous TCU faculty has increased from 30 percent in 1999 to 43 percent in 2006–2007, although their overall proportion is significantly lower than the overall portion of Indigenous students (86 percent) at these institutions. Forty-three percent of AI/AN faculty are full-time, and 57 percent are part-time. Slightly more than half (53 percent) of Indigenous TCU faculty are female. A significant portion of TCU staff (80 percent) and administrators (62 percent) are Indigenous. The majority of non-Native TCU faculty are White (Voorhees, 2003).

Most tribal colleges and universities are two-year institutions. Twelve percent of Native TCU faculty hold associate's degrees, 28 percent bachelor's degrees, 37 percent master's degrees, and 7 percent hold doctoral degrees. Full-time Native faculty are more likely to have higher credentials than part-time faculty. In a national survey comparing TCU faculty to faculty in nontribal, public two-year institutions, Voorhees (2003) found that 45 percent of Native TCU faculty were working toward advanced degrees. In an earlier survey conducted by Clayton and Born (1998), 81 percent of faculty indicated that they would pursue additional college education if it were accessible. Voorhees (2003) points out that a number of Indigenous faculty at TCUs are engaged in tribal language and cultural transmission fields, where qualifications to teach are based primarily on community and life experience and not on graduate credentials (Voorhees, 2003).

According to Voorhees (2003), Native faculty choose to work in TCUs as an explicit commitment to serve their home community or other tribal community and teach Indigenous students. Comparisons between faculty satisfaction in

TCUs and public two-year community colleges indicate that TCU faculty are more content with workload, opportunities for advancement and salary, benefits, and the perceived quality of students. They are less satisfied, however, with available professional opportunities for their spouses or partners and they had less freedom to engage in outside consulting because of the geographic remoteness of most TCUs.

In spite of these findings, recruitment and retention of Indigenous faculty at TCUs is problematic. TCUs are unable to provide salary and benefits that are competitive with other institutions. Faculty salaries at TCUs are significantly lower than faculty salaries at nontribal two-year institutions. The average full-time TCU faculty salary is $37,556 a year (for women, it is $36,337 and for men it is $38,539; AIHEC, 2007). Little Big Horn President Janine Windy Boy stated that, "Working for a tribal college is not unlike entering a religious order . . . You almost have to take vows of poverty in order to serve" (Archambault, 1990). TCU faculty are motivated more by altruism and a desire to serve tribal communities than personal gain (Voorhees, 2003).

TCU faculty typically have an overload of teaching hours; the average number of courses taught per year are 9.5 and the average number of students per course is 15 (AIHEC, 2007). In addition, 87 percent of TCU faculty report having administrative duties and that they spend a great deal of time advising students and providing service to communities that surround the college. The overload of credit hours, administrative duties, advising and service make it difficult for faculty to find time for research or professional development opportunities, although expectations for research and scholarship are increasing in importance (Tippeconnic and McKinney, 2003).

Research and Scholarship at TCUs

Despite the chronic lack of resources and time, some tribal college faculty have found ways to integrate research into their primary role of teaching. Vance (2010) indicated that TCU faculty are more likely to share their work through presentation rather than publication, although it is difficult to quantify how many TCU faculty participate in research and writing, and to what extent, because of limited data collection on scholarship. Examples of scholarship at TCUs include:

At Turtle Mountain Community College a local language scholar worked with a linguistic consultant to write a Chippewa/Cree dictionary. They developed a textbook and drafted 20 stories in the language for use in classes (Ambler and Crazy Bull, 1997).

Both Red Crow and Sinte Gleska University in South Dakota are researching culturally relevant counseling services (Ambler and Crazy Bull, 1997).

At Sinte Gleska, faculty have been developing Lakota language curricula over the years, including the recent completion of a textbook by Albert White Hat (Ambler and Crazy Bull, 1997).

Sinte Gleska offers a cultural resource management degree program.

At Salish Kootenai College, students are interviewing members of the Salish community to develop a Salish language dictionary (Ambler and Crazy Bull, 1997).

Oglala Lakota College and Sinte Gleska, like many Tribal Colleges and Universities, have established archives where they keep written records as well as oral history audio- and videotapes and CDs on subjects such as tribal government, oral histories, music, sacred sites, and dance. The archives serve the colleges and the community.

There have been a handful of funding programs to allow TCU faculty to complete advanced degrees. In 2000, the Bush Foundation funded faculty development in seven different tribal colleges, Haskell Indian Nations University received a U.S. Department of Education Title III grant that allowed five faculty to take one-year sabbaticals to finish their doctorates (Tippeconnic and McKinney, 2003), and in 2003 the Andrew W. Mellon Foundation provided initial funding to help tribal college faculty complete their Ph.D.s. According to a 2008 report from the Council of Graduate Schools, only 58 percent of fellows complete their Ph.D. within ten years (Marchbanks, 2011). TCU doctoral students in the program have emphasized the difference between Western methods of research and traditional Indigenous methods. For TCU faculty, the emphasis of research is on social change, not research for the sake of research or publication (Ambler and Crazy Bull, 1997).

Concluding Thoughts

We must find a way to increase significantly the number of Native faculty who are hired, retained, promoted, and valued in both predominantly White colleges and universities and tribal colleges and universities (Tippeconnic and McKinney, 2003). In their role as scholars, activists, and advocates, Native faculty challenge dominant, racist, and discriminatory scholarship and practices; stimulate research in Indigenous issues; develop and infuse curricula that are inclusive of Native perspectives and scholarship; and assist colleges and universities in recruiting and retaining Native students. With the use of Indigenous knowledge, Native faculty contribute to nation-building efforts, thus improving the social, economic, political and educational conditions of Native and nonnative communities (Tippeconnic and McKinney, 2003).

American Indian and Alaska Native faculty reveal that academic work in service to home communities, and tribal nations more broadly, is what motivates and sustains many through the demands of the job and in spite of oppressive departmental climates that may stereotype and patronize Indigenous scholarship (Faircloth, forthcoming; Fox, 2008). A study by Baez (2011, p. 343) revealed that faculty of color "seek to redefine oppressive structures through service, thus exercising an agency that emerges from the very structures that constrain it. Faculty of color, in particular, may engage in service to promote racial minorities in the academy and elsewhere. This, service, especially which seeks to further social justice, contributes to the redefinition of the academy and society at large." Through their commitment to serving Indigenous communities, American Indian and Alaska Native faculty meet the expectations of the academy but do so on their own terms, in ways that honor Indigenous communities and people.

Where Do We Go From Here?

WE HOPE THAT THIS MONOGRAPH SERVES a number of purposes. First, we hope that the text has offered both a deep and broad overview regarding what is known about American Indian and Alaska Native students and faculty in institutions of higher education. It is evident that Indigenous students and faculty are vastly underrepresented, and we are relatively certain that the reasons, in part, can be tied to a lack of financial support, few role models, cultural incongruities between students' ways of engaging the world and those of the institution, and a lack of academic preparation. These factors are important in understanding why more Indigenous students do not earn degrees. Equally important, from our perspective, is that there are a group of students who are earning degrees. And, although higher education is often marketed (both by the institutions themselves and by their members) as a way for individuals to make better lives for themselves, we believe that many Indigenous students also attend institutions of higher education with the goal of serving others. We want to be clear here, individuals can engage in nation building and benefit individually simultaneously. The issue, from our perspective, is really one of motivation; do the students have a desire to serve their communities in some way, shape, or form or are they motivated solely by making more money and creating a better life for themselves? Our intention here is not to make value judgments. Any time an Indigenous student completes college, it is a victory not only for the individual, but for their communities as well. We are asserting, however, that there seems to be some evidence that students who are motivated by serving others and engaging in a form of nation building are often more likely to complete their degrees than those who do not; these students also engage in improving their communities and nations.

We know that Indigenous students face obstacles in their goal to graduate from college. The retention rate during the first year of college is abysmal and completion rates are often complicated by personal and institutional issues; we also know that there is reason for hope rather than despair, but we believe it will take active engagement by both institutions of higher education and tribal communities to make this work. To this end, we would like to make some research and policy recommendations.

Research Recommendations

Although any number of recommendations for future research could be drawn from what we know about American Indian and Alaska Native higher education, we will highlight a few that are particularly striking. First, research on the experiences of Indigenous college students that addresses the gender, class, and geographic (including urban versus rural as well as on reservation versus off reservation) differences between students is scarce. What does exist tends to generalize across all Indigenous students, even while it appears to be based primarily on work with students from more traditional or reservation communities. Although this work is absolutely important and more of it is needed, we also believe it is necessary to consider the college experiences of Indigenous students from predominantly White and urban and suburban communities, and especially the differences between and among these groups. Understanding the differences across contexts and presenting a range and variation of experiences will allow scholars and institutions an opportunity to address the needs of Indigenous students and their communities.

In a similar vein, very little of the existing work disaggregates data or looks at the variability according to gender or tribal affiliation. James (1995, p. 183) reminds us that we must begin to explore the area of gender. She writes, "There are some indications of differences in educational outcomes for female and male Native American and non-Indian students. Yet gender differences have rarely been examined in studies of Indian education." Although a few studies have examined the higher educational experiences for Indigenous women, next to none have looked at men. Given the enrollment declines for AI/AN men over the past thirty years, this is a critical area for future research. Indeed, we believe that Indigenous men in higher education (and we believe this may extend down to capture Indigenous boys as well) are in crisis. It is imperative that scholars examine the educational plight of Indigenous men and consider ways to increase their enrollment and retention. We are not, however, suggesting that this be done at the expense of continued studies of the experiences of Native girls and women. Both are vital; to place them in competition is a mistake. Indeed, it takes strong men and women to engage in the process of nation building; nations need them standing side by side (both literally and figuratively, in the sense that they need to work together and have similar credentials and complementary skills) to address the challenges they face.

We believe that there must be more longitudinal studies that cover the educational achievement and experiences of Indigenous students in K–16. The problems associated with academic achievement are not inherent to Indigenous peoples, but there is a convergence of policies, schooling systems, and structures that come together with incarceration rates, health concerns, and levels of poverty to almost close the door on most Indigenous youth ever attending, let along graduating from, an institution of higher education. The research and interventions on systems must start early and be sustained. Studies must also be more interdisciplinary in nature; namely, they should employ mixed methods and account for health issues, incarceration rates, other justice-related issues, and institutional types in order to address the needs of Indigenous peoples more fully and adequately. Studies must oversample small populations and contain provisions for gender, geographic, and tribal affiliation differences.

The majority of the research on Indigenous students in higher education also focuses on the direct policy issues of retention and persistence. Tierney (1992, p. 85) notes that, "the scant literature that exists about Native Americans in academe is almost entirely practice-oriented." He identifies three problems with this focus:

1. It never suggests a theoretical orientation that allows the data to be generalizable.

2. It is void of contextual analysis; thus the reader does not learn about the structural or cultural dynamics of situations.
3. It never takes into account the voices of those people under study—American Indians.

Some progress has been made in these areas in the last twenty years, but the field still has a long way to go.

There is, in our minds, a significant need to consider the experiences of Indigenous graduate students. Based on the little data available, it is clear that these students encounter significant resistance and non-Native faculty members who do not understand the students' backgrounds and experiences, are (either intentionally or unintentionally) hostile to their presence, and fail to understand the larger goals of these students. We do not know enough about the pathways to success for these students and best ways to prepare them to become productive faculty, researchers, and contributing members to their communities. If we are to address the lack of role models for undergraduate Indigenous students, it is imperative to consider positive pathways to success for future faculty. From a nation-building perspective, in some ways we are declaring a need for a clear succession strategy. If we think about the fact that many graduate students are seeking additional training and expertise to serve the needs of their constituents better, it is clear that a larger plan must be in place in order to ensure their success. Graduate students may be future faculty. What are institutions doing to assist these students in becoming effective faculty? More focused scholarship on the experiences of graduate students will inform institutions and enable them to meet student needs, and will highlight potential barriers and pitfalls not only for graduate students, but for faculty as well.

We must know more about faculty experiences with students and inside institutions. How do faculty persist? At what cost? What expertise do Native faculty have that is not being utilized to assist both institutions of higher education and tribal nations? We know too little about the day-to-day experiences of Native faculty. A focused examination on this topic will assist in defining how to improve institutions.

Discussion and Implications for Policy

American Indian and Alaska Native education is different from education for any other group because of the unique government-to-government relationship between tribal nations and the federal government, because of the sovereignty and self-determination rights of tribal nations reaffirmed in countless treaties and recent executive orders, and because of the role of the federal government in funding Indigenous educational efforts. The following policy recommendations focus on federal, state, and institutional levels of policy. Each level of policy makers should, in an ideal setting, be aware of the others' moves and initiatives.

American Indians and Alaska Natives have a unique relationship with the federal government—a relationship that places significant responsibility on the federal government to ensure that the sovereignty and self-determination goals of tribal nations are met. The U.S. Commission on Civil Rights has explicitly implicated the federal government in a number of crises affecting American Indians and Alaska Natives:

> *This study reveals that federal funding directed to Native Americans through programs at these agencies has not been sufficient to address the basic and very urgent needs of indigenous peoples. Among the myriad unmet needs are: health care, education, public safety, housing, and rural development [U. S. Commission on Civil Rights, 2003, p. 15].*

The Commission points to the fact that studies and solutions to problems raised for the lives of Indigenous communities must be viewed and addressed through an interdisciplinary lens. The connections between health care, incarceration rates, and public safety should be more fully examined in relation to education in general and higher education in particular. Individuals lead complicated lives; to examine education without interrogating the larger contextual issues in which individuals lead their lives is a mistake. By exploring these areas, individually and in relation to one another, a more holistic picture is painted through which to address potential solutions to the problems at hand.

Importantly, the Commission on Civil Rights provides researchers and policy makers with a set of immediate recommendations and requirements that must be addressed for the sake of Indigenous communities. They write:

Among immediate requirements for increased funding are: infrastructure development, without which tribal governments cannot properly deliver services; tribal courts, which preserve order in tribal communities, provide for restitution of wrongs, and lend strength and validity to other tribal institutions; and tribal priority allowances, which permit tribes to pursue their own priorities and allow tribal governments to respond to the needs of their citizens [U.S. Commission on Civil Rights, 2003, p. 118].

Federal funding for programs that would, in part, ensure some of the unmet needs of tribal nations are met has not yet materialized. Importantly, we would add that individuals and communities must be appropriately trained in order to implement the programs fully to address community needs. We are not simply arguing here that money must be directed to Indigenous communities. We are arguing that appropriate funding and training are necessary to begin the process of remedying the state of Indigenous communities and engaging in tribal nation building.

Funding, however, does continue to be an important aspect of addressing the educational needs of Indigenous communities and the academic achievement of Indigenous students. Almost none of the subprograms for the Office of Indian Education (OIE; part of the U.S. Department of Education) have been funded in the last five years. The OIE's annual $120 million dollar budget spends almost $100 million for formula grants to Indigenous children in the United States. On its face, this is a significant number, but it essentially amounts to $200 per pupil served. The remaining $20 million is aimed at discretionary funding used for research in K–12 schooling and teacher professional development. The U. S. Commission on Civil Rights (2003, p. x) found that, "funding for DOEd's Office of Indian Education (OIE) has remained a relatively small portion of the department's total discretionary budget (ranging from 0.2 to 0.3 percent) between 1998 and 2003. OIE funding has undergone several reductions over the last few decades and, in many years, its budget has failed to account for inflation." OIE needs more funding to meet the needs of Indigenous students by preparing educational professionals. School districts and the federal office need more highly trained individuals to serve Indigenous America. Returning to the qualitative data outlined earlier in this monograph, there must be programs aimed at preparing guidance counselors and other gatekeepers to institutions of higher education who will serve Indigenous students and their educational needs. One way to address the leaking pipeline between high school and college is by having guidance counselors who can adequately guide Indigenous men to higher education. Additionally, it seems to us that funding doctoral studies for future Indigenous faculty could be addressed not only by the Office of Indian Education, but by many private funders as well. A systematic approach to examining and implementing promising practices for graduate students would go a long way to addressing the underrepresentation of Native faculty.

We believe that in the case of examining the experiences of Native peoples, one set of policy makers may not be aware of what other sets are doing. A coordinated effort between different groups will assist in the larger goal of improving the lives of Indigenous peoples. There must be better linkages between the Departments of Interior, Education, and Health and Human Services to meet the needs of Indigenous communities. To this end, we recommend that federal agencies be responsible for knowing what the other is doing related to these issues, and that a point person from each Department be charged with integrating services across departments. Again, the U. S. Commission on Civil Rights (2003, p. x) is worth quoting; they argue: As a group, Native American students are not afforded educational opportunities equal to other American students. They routinely face deteriorating school facilities, underpaid teachers, weak curricula, discriminatory treatment, outdated learning tools, and cultural isolation. As a result, achievement gaps persist with Native American students scoring lower than any other racial/ethnic group in basic levels of reading, math, and history. Native American students are also more likely to drop out. There are structural barriers in place that limit the abilities of Indigenous students to have equitable prospects to achieve academic success. The federal government must meet its obligation to tribal nations and Indigenous children *both* by funding programs *and* by adequately training individuals who provide services to Indigenous communities. Importantly, we believe that large-scale databases used in the Departments of Education, Health, Justice, and Interior can and should be linked. This linkage will provide researchers with the necessary tools to begin examining the links between health, education, and the general welfare of Native peoples. Having a fuller picture of the structural barriers present allows ways to explore solutions to the problems encountered by Indigenous peoples.

Ironically, not long after President Bush signed into effect the 2004 Executive Order, his Secretary of Education, Margaret Spellings, moved the Office of Indian Education from its position where it reported directly to the Deputy Secretary of Education and was a more autonomous unit; instead, she placed it in the Office of Elementary and Secondary Education. The reshuffling process wherein Secretary Spellings imposed more of a bureaucratic burden on the officers in OIE may have set the office back by ten years. Simply put, the executive branch argued (in the Executive Order) for greater autonomy and better relationships between the U.S. government and tribal nations, and then acted in a way to cut off the march toward self-determination by moving the OIE. Placing OIE back into its semiautonomous position where it had greater freedom to implement its important programs would greatly enhance its work in meeting the educational needs of Indigenous children.

We believe that the government's failure to meet its obligation is systemic and must be addressed systemically. A task force comprised of individuals involved in the fields of health, education, and community development as well as members from tribal nations must be formed to establish a step-by-step process to address the crisis. Indigenous communities must have a seat at the table to address the systematic nature of the federal government's failures in productive ways that the communities can begin to own for themselves. More specifically, we think there must be greater accountability by the federal government to meet its responsibilities to tribal communities and their citizens. The task force should have access to relevant data and individuals who can analyze the data systematically and quickly in order to grade the federal government's responsiveness to the needs of Indigenous communities and their children. Part of this report card should also include an examination of where educational and health services are breaking down. The task force should prepare an annual report that is publicly distributed with recommendations to Congress for future funding.

We agree with the National Center for Public Policy and Higher Education who writes, "states are the decision-making entities historically responsible for higher education policy, and they remain the ones best situated to frame a broad public policy agenda for all of education, with the greatest probability of success in maintaining focus and sustaining policy" (National Center for Public Policy and Higher Education, 2005, p. 1a). Tribal governments are well positioned to address the educational needs of their students. In order for tribes to build educational capacity, States must recognize tribal authority over the education of their students and consult with tribes to transfer education programs, consult with Indian tribes in the development of Title I plans, and authorize tribes to receive grants to participate in school improvement, innovative practices, and dropout prevention programs (Tribal Education Departments National Assembly [TEDNA], 2011; National Indian Education Association [NIEA], 2011). States should also be required to disaggregate American Indian student information by tribal membership, and generally incorporate Indian tribes and tribal education agencies into the programs authorized in each section of the ESEA (TEDNA, 2011). To this end, states must become more active in ensuring that American Indians and Alaska Natives from their states have adequate access to institutions of higher education. State offices of education must be particularly diligent that all children and youth are receiving adequate educational opportunities that will allow them to attend college if they so choose. The idea that in 2011 there are still high schools that lack the course offerings to make their valedictorians eligible for college is disheartening and inequitable to a point of being a human rights violation.

As states become more invested in providing funding for students, they must more closely examine the ways they are conceptualizing merit-based funding. "Because need-based financial aid has not kept pace with tuition increases, low and middle income students are slowly being priced out of colleges. Rising unmet financial need means that over 200,000 college-qualified students annually are unable to afford to go to college—even at their local community colleges" (The National Center for Public Policy and Higher Education, 2005,

p. 2a). If Heller (2005) and St. John (2004) are correct, these programs continue to fund students who would have attended college anyway. States must rethink what counts as merit and begin to explore ways that they may assist Indigenous children in educational achievement and attainment at all levels. This is especially true at the level of postsecondary education.

States must work closely with federal agencies to ensure that federal monies are being appropriately allocated to the students they were originally earmarked to serve. In an era of accountability, we must assess whether the needs of underrepresented students are being met, and those individuals and agencies charged with this work must be accountable to the federal government and state constituencies.

Discussion and Implications for Institutional Practice

Finally, institutions of higher education themselves must address institutional-specific issues related to the recruitment, retention, and graduation of Indigenous students. Institutions must assess how they recruit Indigenous students. Are there requirements in place for students to verify their tribal enrollment, or do applicants self-identify? Do admissions criteria unintentionally privilege particular students? Every institution with an Indigenous population of more than 3 percent should engage in a thorough campus climate study that is designed with input from Indigenous faculty, staff, and students. The climate at these institutions may contribute to the fact that so many AI/AN students leave after their first year of college. Institutions must ask themselves: Once Indigenous students arrive on campus, what are their experiences, what leads to their success, and what could the institution be doing differently to meet their needs better? These climate studies will surely point to the level of hostility toward Indigenous people.

Beyond climate studies, however, we believe that institutions should engage tribal nations in conversations aimed at meeting the needs of the nations. If the climate at institutions is chilly, how can this be addressed? Additionally, tribal nations can guide and direct institutions in the role of research that may address the needs of the nations. This can lead to answering questions like: How are health issues, like obesity and diabetes, being addressed in meaningful ways that will simultaneously allow researchers to conduct much needed research and serve the needs of communities? How can teacher preparation be structured so that it both prepares teachers to meet the needs of diverse students, including Native students, and provides a healthy and productive space for Native preservice teachers to engage issues relevant to their communities? How can sociology and anthropology departments conduct sensitive research, informed by the disciplinary norms that will not be rooted in deficit orientations, but in ones that are focused on strengthening communities and building places of promise? In short, institutions can—indeed, they must—reconsider the ways that they do business regarding Indigenous students, faculty, and communities. Tribal nations would do well to consider what they may draw from meaningful relationships with institutions of higher education.

In conclusion, it is imperative that researchers, policy makers, and those working in colleges and universities consider the long-term effects of hostile educational practices for Indigenous peoples. We believe that a nation-building approach to higher education is one route toward better understanding places of possibility and hope. We know too well why students are not graduating from colleges and universities, but know very little about promising practices and sites of success. In 1916, Seneca scholar A.C. Parker wrote, "Human beings have a primary right to an intellectual life, but civilization has swept down upon groups of Indians and, by destroying their relationships to nature, blighted or banished their intellectual life, and left a group of people mentally confused . . . The Indians must have a thought-world given back. Their intellectual world must have direct relation to their world of responsible acts and spontaneous experiences" (Parker, 1916, p. 258). We don't believe that Indigenous peoples, through the process of nation building, are demanding and taking their thought worlds back from the process of colonization. We believe that institutions of higher education offer possibilities and that by working with researchers and communities, they can change the tide that batters Native students, their communities, and tribal nations against the shoreline to one that is favorable, useful, and productive.

Notes

1. Throughout this text, we use American Indian, Alaska Native, Native, and Indigenous students interchangeably. We intentionally capitalize Indigenous to demonstrate the political status of the term and recognize the sovereign status of the peoples to whom it refers.
2. The boarding-school era, which began in 1879, was largely initiated by a former Army soldier named William Pratt. Pratt sold Congress on his plan by offering a glimmer of hope that the boarding-school process would rid Indigenous peoples of the bad influences of communal living, long hair, and uncivilized behaviors. He noted that the goal of the schools and process was to "kill the Indian and save the man."
3. Deloria (1976, p. 28) is very helpful here in moving beyond notions of focusing on *sovereignty* as just a legal/political concept. He writes, "'Sovereignty' is a useful word to describe the process of growth and awareness that characterizes a group of people working toward and achieving maturity. If it is restricted to a legal–political context, then it becomes a limiting concept, which serves to prevent solutions. The legal–political context is structured in an adversary situation which precludes both understanding and satisfactory resolution of difficulties and should be considered as a last resort, not as a first instance in which human problems and relationships are to be seen." Our arguments in this short text point to the usefulness of addressing sovereignty more broadly.

References

Achieve, Inc. (2009). Closing the expectations gap: Fourth annual 50-state progress report of the alignment of high school policies with the demands of college and careers. Achieve/American Diploma Project Network. Retrieved March, 2009, from www.Achieve.org.

ACT (2007). *Rigor at risk: Reaffirming quality in the high school curriculum.* Iowa City, IA: ACT.

ACT (2010a). *Mind the gaps: How college readiness narrows achievement gaps in college success.* Iowa City, IA: ACT.

ACT (2010b). *The condition of college and career readiness 2010.* Iowa City, IA: ACT.

Adams, D. W. (1998). Fundamental considerations: The deep meaning of Native American schooling, 1880–1990. *Harvard Educational Review, 58*(1), 1–25.

Adams, J. (2002, Dec. 23). For Time magazine, sovereignty 101. *Indian Country Today.*

Adams, K. B. (1988). Order in the courts: Resolution of tribal–state criminal jurisdictional disputes. *Tulsa Law Journal, 24*(1), 89–116.

Adams, N. (1992). My grandmother and the snake. In A. Garrod and C. Larrimore (Eds.), *First person, first peoples: Native American college graduates tell their life stories.* Ithaca, NY: Cornell University Press.

Adelman, C. (1999). *Answers in the tool box: Academic intensity, attendance patterns and bachelor's degree attainment.* Washington, DC: U.S. Department of Education, Office of Educational Research and Improvement.

Adelman, C. (2002). The relationship between urbanicity and educational outcomes. In W. G. Tierney and L. S. Hagedorn (Eds.), *Increasing access to college: Extending possibilities for all students* (pp. 15–34). New York: State University of New York.

Adelman, C. (2006). *The toolbox revisited: Paths to degree completion from high school through college.* Washington, D.C.: U.S. Department of Education, 2006.

Advisory Committee on Student Financial Assistance (2001). *Access Denied, Restoring The Nation's Commitment to Equal Educational Opportunity.* Washington, DC: Advisory Committee on Student Financial Assistance.

Agbo, S. A. (2001). Enhancing success in American Indian students: Participatory research at Akwesasne as part of the development of a culturally relevant curriculum. *Journal of American Indian Education, 40*(1), 31–56.

Akoto, K. A. (1992). *Nationbuilding: Theory and practice in Afrikan centered education.* Washington, DC: Pan Afrikan World Institute.

Alaska Native Knowledge Network. (1998). Retrieved, January 30, 2012, from http://www.ankn.uaf.edu/publications/culturalstandards.pdf.

Alfred, T.G.R. (1995). *Heeding the voices of our ancestors: Kahnawake Mohawk politics and the rise of native nationalism.* Don Mills, Canada: Oxford University Press Canada.

Alfred, T.G.R. (1999). *Peace, power, righteousness: An indigenous manifesto.* Don Mills, Canada: Oxford University Press.

Alfred, T.G.R. (2005). *Wasase: Indigenous pathways of action and freedom.* Peterborough, Canada: Broadview Press.

Almanac of Higher Education. (2011). *Chronicle of higher education.* Retrieved January 30, 2012, from http://chronicle.com/article/Almanac-2011-Access-and/128457/.

Almeida, D. (1997). The hidden half: A history of Native American women's education. *Harvard Educational Review, 67*(4), 757–771.

Ambler, M., and Crazy Bull, C. (1997). Survey: Tribal colleges deeply involved in research. *Tribal College, IX*(1), 12.

American Indian College Fund. (2004). *Annual report: Educating the mind and spirit.* Denver, CO: American Indian College Fund.

American Indian Higher Education Consortium (AIHEC). (1999). *Tribal colleges: An introduction.* Washington, DC: American Indian Higher Education Consortium.

American Indian Higher Education Consortium (AIHEC). (2000). *Tribal college contributions to local economic development.* Washington, DC: American Indian Higher Education Consortium.

American Indian Higher Education Consortium (AIHEC). (2001). *TCUs as engaged institutions.* Washington, DC: American Indian Higher Education Consortium.

American Indian Higher Education Consortium (AIHEC). (2007). *AIHEC AIMS Fact Book 2007. Tribal Colleges and Universities Report.* Washington, DC: American Indian Higher Education Consortium.

Antonio, A. L. (2000). Faculty of color and scholarship transformed: New arguments for diversifying faculty. *Diverse Digest, 3*(2), 6–7.

Archambault, D. (1990). Washington roulette: Playing—and winning—by the rules of politics. *Tribal College, II*(1), 5.

Archibald, J. (Ed.). (2001). Sharing Aboriginal knowledge and Aboriginal ways of knowing. *Canadian Journal of Native Education, 25*(1), 1–89.

Astin, A., and L. Oseguera. (2004). The declining "equity" of American higher education. *Review of Higher Education, 27*(3), 321–341.

Atalay, S. (2006). Indigenous archaeology as decolonizing practice. *American Indian Quarterly, 30*(3/4), 280–310.

Auerbach, S. (2002). "Why do they give the good classes to some and not to others?" Latino parent narratives of struggle in a college access program. *Teachers College Record, 104*(7), 1369–1392.

Austin, R. (2005). Perspectives of American Indian nation parents and leaders. *New Directions for Student Services, 109*, 41–48.

Bad Wound, E. (1991). Teaching to empower: Tribal colleges must promote leadership and self determination in their reservations. *Tribal College, III*(1), 15.

Baez, B. (2011). Race-related service and faculty of color: Conceptualizing critical agency in academe. In S. R. Harper and S. Hurtado (Eds.), *Racial and ethnic diversity in higher education*. ASHE Reader Series (3rd ed., pp. 343–360). Boston, MA: Pearson Learning Solutions.

Baker, T. L., and Vélez, W. (1996). Access to and opportunity in postsecondary education in the United States: A review. *Sociology of Education, 69*, 82–101.

Ballew, R. L. (1996). *The experience of Native American women obtaining doctoral degrees in the psychology at traditional American universities* (Unpublished doctoral dissertation). The University of Tennessee, Knoxville.

Barker, J. (2005). *Sovereignty matters: Locations of contestation and possibility in indigenous struggles for self-determination*. Lincoln, NE: University of Nebraska Press.

Barnhardt, R., and Kawagley, A. O. (2005). Indigenous knowledge systems and Alaska Native ways of knowing. *Anthropology and Education Quarterly, 36*(1), 8–23.

Barnhardt, R., and Laughlin, E. (2005, May 18). New school provides strong foundation for all students. *Fairbanks Daily News-Miner*. Retrieved January 30, 2012, from http://www.ankn.uaf.edu/NPE/EKCS/News1.html.

Bartlett, D. L., and Steele, J. B. (2002, December 16). *Indian Casinos: Wheel of Misfortune — Who Gets the Money? (Part 1)*. Retrieved January 30, 2012, from http://www.barlettandsteele.com/journalism/time_casino_1.php.

Bass, W. P. (1971). Formal education of American Indians. *Journal of Research and Developmental Education, 4*, 21–32.

Battiste, M. (2000). Maintaining Aboriginal identity, language, and culture in modern society. In M. Battiste (Ed.), *Reclaiming Indigenous voice and vision* (pp. 192–208). Vancouver, Canada: UBC Press.

Battiste, M. (2002). *Indigenous knowledge and pedagogy in first nations education: A literature review with recommendations*. Ottawa, Canada: Indian and Northern Affairs Canada.

Battiste, M., and Barman, J. (1995). Introduction. In M. Battiste and J. Barman (Eds.), *First Nations education in Canada: The circle unfolds*. Vancouver, Canada: University of British Columbia Press.

Bell, N. (2011). *Graduate Enrollment and Degrees: 2000 to 2010*. Washington, DC: Council of Graduate Schools.

Benally, S. (2004, March). *Serving American Indian students: Participation in accelerated learning opportunities*. Western Interstate Commission for Higher Education. Retrieved May 6, 2004 from http://www.wiche.edu/Policy/WCALO/Publications.asp.

Beatty, A., Greenwood, M.C.R., and Linn, R. (Eds.) (1999). *Myths and tradeoffs: The roles of tests in undergraduate admissions.* Washington, DC: National Academy.

Benham, M.K.P., and Stein, W. J. (Eds.). (2003). *The renaissance of American Indian higher education.* Mahwah, NJ: Lawrence Erlbaum.

Benjamin, D. P., Chambers, S., and Reiterman, G. (1993). A focus on American Indian college persistence. *Journal of American Indian Education, 32*(2), 24–40.

Besaw, A., and others (2004). *The context and meaning of family strengthening in Indian America.* A report to the Annie E. Casey Foundation by The Harvard Project on American Indian Economic Development. Washington, DC.

Blain, J. A. (2010). *(Post)development and food sovereignty for California Indian nation building* (Unpublished master's thesis). University of California–Davis.

Bowen, W. G., and Bok, D. (1998). *The shape of the river: Long-term consequences of considering race in college and university admissions.* Princeton, NJ: Princeton University.

Bowker, A. (1992). The American Indian female dropout. *Journal of American Indian Education, 31*(3), 3–20.

Boyer, P. (2005). To be, or not to be? TCUs probe identity questions as they 'indigenize' their institutions. *Tribal College, 16*(3), 11.

Brade, C., Duncan, K. A., and Sokal, L. (2003). The path to education in a Canadian Aboriginal context. *Canadian Journal of Native Education, 27*(2), 235–249.

Bray, B. (1992). Refuse to kneel. In A. Garrod and C. Larimore (Eds.), *First person, first peoples: Native American college graduates tell their life stories* (pp. 27–40). Ithaca, NY: Cornell University Press.

Brayboy, B. M. (1999). *Climbing the ivy: Examining the experiences of academically successful Native American Indian students in two Ivy League universities* (Unpublished doctoral dissertation). University of Pennsylvania, Philadelphia.

Brayboy, B. M. (2002, April). *Tribal critical race theory in higher education.* Presented at the Annual Meeting of the American Educational Research Association, New Orleans, Louisiana.

Brayboy, B.M.J. (2004). Hiding in the ivy: American Indian students and visibility in elite educational settings. *Harvard Educational Review, 74*(2), 125–152.

Brayboy, B.M.J. (2005a). Toward a tribal critical race theory in education. *The Urban Review, 37*(5), 425–446.

Brayboy, B.M.J. (2005b). Transformational resistance and social justice: American Indians in Ivy League universities. *Anthropology and Education Quarterly, 36*(3), 193–211.

Brayboy, B.M.J. (2006). *Indigenous men in higher education.* Washington, DC: The Dellums Commission and the Joint Center on Economic and Political Studies.

Brayboy, B.M.J. (2010, October 29). The current status of minority males in higher education: A pending crisis. Participant, Institute on Teaching and Mentoring, Tampa, FL.

Brayboy, B.M.J., and Maughan, E. (2009). Indigenous knowledges and the story of the bean. *Harvard Educational Review, 79*(1), 1–21.

Breinig, J. (2003). Doing everything and nothing, a first year Experience. *American Indian Quarterly, 27(1/2)*, 103–112.

Brown, L. D. (2000). *American Indians in higher education: One student's story* (Unpublished doctoral dissertation). Iowa State University, Ames.

Buckley, A. (1997). *Threads of nations: American Indian graduate and professional students* (ERIC ED 444 771).

Burkhart, B. Y. (2004). What coyote and Thales can teach us: An outline of American Indian epistemology. In A. Waters (Ed.), *American Indian thought: Philosophical essays* (pp. 15–26). Malden, MA: Blackwell Publishing.

Cabrera, A. F., and La Nasa, S. N. (2000). Understanding the college-choice process. *New Directions for Institutional Research, 107,* 5–22.

Calhoun, J. A. (2003). "It's just a social obligation. You could say 'No'!": Cultural and religious barriers of American Indian faculty in the academy. *American Indian Quarterly, 27*(1/2), 132–154.

Campbell, A. E. (2007). Retaining American Indian/Alaskan Native students in higher education: A case study of one partnership between the Tohono O'odham Nation and Pima Community College, Tucson, AZ. *Journal of American Indian Education, 26*(2), 19–29.

Campbell, L., Egawa, K., and Wortman, G. (2003). *Increasing the achievement of Native American youth at early college high schools.* New Horizons for Learning. Retrieved Sept. 23, 2008 from, http://www.newhorizons.org/strategies/multicultural/campbell_egawa_wortman.htm.

Card, D., and Rothstein, J. (2007). Racial segregation and the Black–White test score gap. *Journal of Public Economics, 91*(11/12), 2158–2184.

Carney, C. M. (1999). *Native American higher education in the United States.* New Brunswick, NJ: Transaction Publishers.

Carroll, R. E. (1978). A study of Haskell students: Academic performance and cultural marginality. *Journal of American Indian Education, 18*(1), 11–16.

Castagno, A. E. (2003). *(Re)Contextualizing Indian higher education: A qualitative study of Indigenous women at a predominantly White university* (Unpublished master's thesis). University of Wisconsin, Madison.

Castagno, A., and Lee, S. (2007). Native mascots, ethnic fraud, and interest convergence: A critical race theory perspective on higher education. *Equity and Excellence in Education, 40*(1), 3–13.

Castagno, A. E., and Brayboy, B.M.J. (2008). Culturally responsive schooling for indigenous youth: A review of the literature. *Review of Educational Research, 78*(4), 941–993.

Center for Native Education (2009). Fact sheet. Portland, OR: Center for Native Education. Retrieved from http://www.centerfornativeed.org/pdf/ cne_factsheet.pdf

Champagne, D. (2004). Education for nation-building. *Cultural Survival Quarterly, 2/*(4), 35.

Champagne, D. (2007). In search of theory and method in American Indian studies. *American Indian Quarterly, 31*(3), 353–372.

Champagne, D. (2008). From first nations to self-government. *American Behavioral Scientist, 51*(12), 1672–1693.

Chavers, D. (2002). *Indian students and college preparation.* Albuquerque, NM: Catching the Dream.

Clayton, D., and Born, D. (1998). *Report to the Bush Foundation on tribal college faculty development need.* Duluth: University of Minnesota.

Cleary, L. M., and Peacock, T. (1997). Disseminating American Indian educational research through stories: A case against academic discourse. *Journal of American Indian Education, 37*(1), 7–15.

Coffey, W., and Tsosie, R. (2001). Rethinking the tribal sovereignty doctrine: Cultural sovereignty and the collective future of Indian nations. *Stanford Law and Policy Review, 12*(2), 191–221.

Coggins, K., Williams, E., and Radin, N. (1997). The traditional tribal values of Ojibwa parents and the school performance of their children: An exploratory study. *Journal of American Indian Education, 36*(3), 1–15.

Cohen, A. M., and Brawer, F. (2003). *The American community college.* San Francisco, CA: Jossey Bass.

Coin, J. (2003). Nation building lessons in the Hoopa Valley. *Indian Country Today, 23*(13), A6.

College Board (2011, February 9). *The 7th Annual AP Report to the Nation.* College Board. Retrieved from http://apreport.collegeboard.org/sites/default/files/downloads/pdfs/AP_RTN_2011.pdf

Cook-Lynn, E. (2001). *Anti-Indianism in modern America: A voice from Tatekeya's Earth.* Urbana, IL: University of Illinois Press.

Cornell, S. (1987). *American Indians, American dreams, and the meaning of success.* Malcolm Weiner Center for Social Policy: Harvard Project on American Indian development, John F. Kennedy School of Government, Harvard University, Cambridge, MA.

Cornell, S., and Kalt, J. P. (Eds.) (1992). *What can tribes do? Strategies and institutions in American Indian economic development.* Los Angeles, CA: American Indian Studies Center at the University of California, Los Angeles.

Cornell, S., and Kalt, J. P. (1998). Sovereignty and nation-building: The development challenges in Indian country today. *American Culture and Research Journal, 22,* 187–214.

Cornell, S., and Kalt, J. P. (2003). Sovereignty and nation-building: The development challenge in Indian country today. *American Indian Culture and Research Journal, 22*(3), 187–214.

Cornell, S., and Kalt, J. P. (2006). *Two approaches to economic development on American Indian reservations: One works, the other doesn't.* Harvard Project on American Indian Economic Development and the Native Nations Institute for Leadership, Management, and Policy on behalf of the Arizona Board of Regents, Tucson, AZ.

Cornell, S., and Kalt, J. P. (2010). *American Indian self-determination: The political economy of a policy that works.* HKS Faculty Research Working Paper Series. Cambridge, MA: Harvard University.

Cross, W. T. (1991). Pathway to the professoriate; the American Indian faculty pipeline. *Journal of American Indian Education, 30*(2), 13–24.

Crum, S. (1989). The idea of an Indian college or university in the twentieth century America before the formation of the Navajo community college in 1968. *Tribal College Journal of American Indian Higher Education, 1*(2), 20–23.

Cunningham, A. F., McSwain, C., and Keselman, Y. (2007). *The path of many journeys: The benefits of higher education for Native people and communities.* A report by the Institute for Higher Education Policy, in collaboration with the American Indian Higher Education Consortium and the American Indian College Fund. Retrieved March, 2007, from www.ihep.org.

Dana-Sacco, G. (2010). The Indigenous researcher as individual and collective: Building a research practice ethic within the context of Indigenous languages. *American Indian Quarterly, 34*(1), 61–82.

de la Torre, J. (2004). In the trenches: A critical look at the isolation of American Indian political practices in the nonempirical social science of political science. In D. A. Mihesuah and A. C. Wilson (Eds.), *Indigenizing the academy: Transforming scholarship and empowering communities* (pp. 174–190). Lincoln: University of Nebraska Press.

Deloria, V., and Lytle, C. M. (1983). *American Indians, American justice* (1st ed.). Austin, TX: University of Texas Press.

Deloria, V., and Wildcat, D. R. (2001). *Power and place: Indian education in America.* Golden, CO: Fulcrum.

Deloria, V., Jr. (1976). *A Better Day for Indians.* New York: Field Foundation.

Deloria, V., Jr. (1988). *Custer died for your sins: An Indian manifesto.* Norman, OK: University of Oklahoma.

Deloria, V., Jr. (2004). Marginal and submarginal. In D. A. Mihesuah and A. C. Wilson (Eds.), *Indigenizing the academy: Transforming scholarship and empowering communities* (pp. 16–30). Lincoln, NE: University of Nebraska Press.

Demmert, W. G. (2001). *Improving academic performance among Native American students: A review of research literature.* Charleston, WV: ERIC Clearinghouse on Rural Education and Small Schools.

DeVoe, J. F., and Darling-Churchill, K. E. (2008). *Status and trends in the education of American Indians and Alaska natives: 2008. (NCES 2008–08).* Washington, DC: National Center for Education Statistics, Institute of Education Sciences, U.S. Department of Education.

Deyhle, D. (1992). Constricting failure and maintaining cultural identity: Navajo and Ute school leavers. *Journal of American Indian Education, 31*(2), 24–47.

Deyhle, D. (1995). Navajo youth and Anglo racism: Cultural integrity and resistance. *Harvard Educational Review, 65*(3), 403–444.

Deyhle, D. (1998). From break dancing to heavy metal: Navajo youth, resistance, and identity. *Youth and Society, 30*(1), 3–31.

Deyhle, D., and Swisher, K. (1997). Research in American Indian and Alaska native education: From assimilation to self-determination. *Review of Research in Education, 22,* 113–194.

Dhamoon, R., and Abu-Laban, Y. (2009). Dangerous (internal) foreigners and nation-building: The case of Canada. *International Political Science Review, 30*(2), 163–183.

Duchene, M. (1988). Giant law, giant education, and ant: A story about racism and Native Americans. *Harvard Educational Review, 58*(3), 354–362.

Engle, J., and Tinto, V. (2008). *Moving beyond access: College success for low-income, first-generation students*. Washington, DC: The Pell Institute for the Study of Opportunity in Higher Education.

EPE Research Center. (2010). Bethesda, MD: Editorial Projects in Education. Retrieved January 30, 2012, from http://www.edweek.org/media/ew/qc/2011/16sos.h30.k12.pdf.

Etzioni, A. (2009/2010). Bottom-up nation building. *Policy Review, 158,* 51–62.

Federal Register (2004, May 5). Executive Order 13336: American Indian Alaska Native Education. *Federal Register, 69*(87). Retrieved January 8, 2012, from http://edocket.access.gpo.gov/2004/pdf/04-10377.pdf.

Faircloth, S. C. (2009). Re-visioning the future of education for Native youth in rural schools and communities. *Journal of Research in Rural Education, 24*(9), 1–4.

Faircloth, S. C. (Forthcoming). Seeking more than balance: An American Indian female scholar's attempt to navigate the perceived work-life divide. In J. Marshall (Ed.), *Juggling Flaming Chainsaws: Faculty in Educational Leadership Try to Balance Work and Life*. Charlotte, NC: Information AgePublishing.

Faircloth, S. C., and Tippeconnic, J. W., III. (2010). *The dropout/graduation crisis among American Indian and Alaska Native students: Failure to respond places the future of Native peoples at risk*. Published report in collaboration with the Civil Rights Project at UCLA and the Center for the Study of Leadership in American Indian Education at Penn State University.

Falk, D., and Aitken, L. (1984). Promoting retention among American Indian college students. *Journal of American Indian Education, 23*(2), 24–31.

Fann, A. (2005). *Forgotten students: Native high school narratives on college access* (Unpublished doctoral dissertation). University of California–Los Angeles.

Fassinger, R.E. (2008). Workplace diversity and public policy: Challenges and opportunities for psychology. *American Psychologist, 63(4),* 252–268.

Fisher, S. (1994). *Stress in academic life: the mental assembly line*. Buckingham, UK: Society for Research into Higher Education & Open University Press.

Fitzgerald, B. K., and Delaney, J. A. (2002). Educational opportunity in America. In D. E. Heller (Ed.), *Conditions of access: Higher education for lower-income students*. Westport, CT: American Council on Education/Preager Series on Higher Education.

Fixico, D. (1995). American Indians (the minority of minorities) and higher education. In B. Bowser, T. Jones, and G. A. Young (Eds.), *Toward the multicultural university* (pp. 103–124). Westport, CT: Praeger.

Fox, M.J.T. (2008). American Indian women in academics: The joys and challenges. *Journal About Women in Higher Education, 1,* 202–220.

Freeman, K. (1997). Increasing African Americans' participation in higher education. *Journal of Higher Education, 68*(5), 523–550.

Freeman, K. (1999, March). The race factor in African Americans' college choice. *Urban Education, 34*(1), 4–25.

Frickey, P. P. (1997). Adjudication and its discontents: Coherence and conciliation in federal Indian law. *Harvard Law Review, 110*(8), 1754–1784.

Garrod, A., and Larimore, C. (1997). *First person, first peoples: Native American college gradu-ates tell their life stories*. Ithaca, NY: Cornell University Press.

Gay, G. (2004). Navigating marginality en route to the professoriate: Graduate students of color learning and living in academia. *International Journal of Qualitative Studies in Education, 17*(2), 265–288.

Government Accountability Office (GAO) (2006, January). *Telecommunications: Challenges to Assessing and Improving Telecommunications for Native Americans in Tribal Lands*. Wash-ington, DC: United States Government Accountability Office. GAO-06-189.

Gilmore, P., Smith, D., and Kairaiuak, A. (1997). Resisting diversity: An Alaskan case of institutional struggle. In M. Fine, L. Weis, L. Powell, and M. Wong (Eds.), *Off white: Readings on race, power, and society* (pp. 90–99). New York, NY: Routledge.

Glipo, A., and Pascual, F. G. (2005). *Food sovereignty framework: Concept and historical con-text*. Retrieved from http://tinyurl.com/3t73bdt.

Goldberg-Ambrose, C. (1997). *Plating tail feathers: Tribal survival and Public Law 280*. Los Angeles, CA: American Indian Studies Center.

Gonzalez, R. G. (2008). From creation to cultural resistance and expansion: Research on American Indian higher education. In J. C. Smart (Ed.), *Higher education: Handbook of theory and research* (pp. 299–327). New York: Agathon Press.

Grande, S. (2004). *Red pedagogy: Native American social and political thought*. New York: Rowman and Littlefield.

Great Plains Tribal Chairman's Association (2010). *Broadband Initiatives Program and Broad-band Technology Opportunities Program Joint Request for Information*. Rapid City, SD: Great Plains Tribal Chairman's Association. Retrieved from http://www.ntia.doc.gov/files/ntia/broadbandgrants/comments/rfi2/GPTCA%20RFI%20BIP-BTOP%20Broadband%20Funds%20-%20Policy%20Recommendations.pdf.

Greene, J. P., and Forster, G. (2003, September). *Public high school graduation and college readiness rates in the United States. Education working paper no. 3*. New York: Manhattan Institute for Policy Research.

Guillory, R., and Wolverton, M. (2008). It's about family: Native American student persis-tence in higher education. *Journal of Higher Education, 79*(1), 58–87.

Hanna, R. M. (2005). *Attainment of doctoral degree for American Indian and Alaska Native women* (Unpublished doctoral dissertation). University of Central Florida, Orlando, FL.

Hansen, T. (2008). Innovative program results in educational success for Native students. *Indian Country Today Education, 12–14.*

Harvard Project on American Indian Economic Development (HPAIED). (2008). *The state of Native nations: Conditions under U.S. policies of self-determination*. New York: Oxford University Press.

Havighurst, R. (1981). Indian education: Accomplishments of the last decade. *Phi Delta Kappan, 62*(5), 329–331.

Hawkins, D. (1993). Pre-college counselors challenged for misadvising minorities: Full array of options not always explored. *Black Issues in Higher Education, 10*(1), 14–15.

HeavyRunner, I., and DeCelles, R. (2002). Family education model: Meeting the student retention challenge. *Journal of American Indian Education, 41*(2), 29–37.

Heionen, N. L. (2002). *Evaluation of critical identification and coping strategies as predictors of percentage of graduate degree completed by American Indian students* (Unpublished doctoral dissertation). Los Angeles, CA: California School of Professional Psychology.

Heller, D. E. (2005). *Need and merit in financial aid.* Paper presented at the National Scholarship Providers Association Annual Conference.

Heller, D. E. (1999). The effects of tuition and state financial aid on public college enrollment. *Review of Higher Education, 23*(1), 65–90.

Helton, T. (2003/2004). Nation building in Indian country: The Blackfoot constitutional review. *The Kansas Journal of Law and Public Policy, 13,* 1–57.

Henning, D. (1999). *American Indian perspectives of doctoral program experiences and completion* (Unpublished doctoral dissertation). New Mexico State University.

Herzig, A. H. (2004). Becoming mathematicians: Women and students of color choosing and leaving doctoral mathematics. *Review of Educational Research, 74*(2), 171–214.

Hill, N. S. (1991). A college intervention program that works. *Change, 23*(2), 3–5.

Hoover, J., and Jacobs, C. (1992). A survey of American Indian college students: Perceptions toward their study skills/college life. *Journal of American Indian Education, 32*(1), 21–29.

Hossler, D., Braxton, J., and Coopersmith, G. (1989). Understanding student college choice. In J. Smart (Ed.), *Higher education: Handbook of theory and research* (Vol. 5, pp. 231–238). New York: Agathon Press.

Hossler, D., Schmit, J., and Vesper, N. (1998). *Going to college: How social, economic, and educational factors influence the decisions students make.* Baltimore, MD: John Hopkins University.

Houser, S. (1991). Building institutions across cultural boundaries: Management of Indian institutions. *Tribal College, 2*(3), 11–17.

Hunt, B., and Harrington, C. F. (2008). The impending education crisis for American Indians: Higher education at the crossroads. *Journal of Multicultural, Gender and Minority Studies, 2,* 1–11.

Hunter, A. A. (2004). Teaching Indigenous cultural resource management. In D. A. Mihesuah and A. C. Wilson (Eds.), *Indigenizing the academy: Transforming scholarship and empowering communities* (pp. 160–173). Lincoln, NE: University of Nebraska Press.

Hurtado, S., Inkelas, K. K., Briggs, C., and Rhee, B. S. (1997). Difference in college access and choice among racial/ethnic groups: Identifying continuing barriers. *Research in Higher Education, 38,* 43–74.

Innes, R.A. (2009). "Wait a second, who are you anyways?: The insider/outsider debate and American Indian studies." *American Indian Quarterly, 33*(4), 440–461.

Institute of Education Statistics. (2004). The condition of education. *National Center for Education Statistics.* Washington, DC: U.S. Department of Education.

Jackson, A. P., and Smith, S. A. (2001). Postsecondary transitions among Navajo students. *Journal of American Indian Education, 40*(2), 28–47.

James, K. (1995). "School Achievement and Dropout Among Anglo and Indian Females and Males: A Comparative Examination," *American Indian and Research Journal, 19*(3), 183.

James, K. (2004). Corrupt state university: The organizational psychology of native experience in higher education. In D.A. Mihesuah and A. C. Wilson, (Eds.), *Indigenizing the Academy: Transforming Scholarship and Empowering Communities* (pp. 48–68). Lincoln: University of Nebraska Press.

Jayakumar, U. M., Howard, T. C., and Allen, W. (2009). Racial privilege in the professoriate: An exploration of campus climate, retention, and satisfaction. *The Journal of Higher Education, 80*(5), 538–563.

Jennings, M. (2004). *Alaska Native political leadership and higher education: One university, two universes.* Walnut Creek, CA: Altamira Press.

Jorgensen, M. (2007). *Rebuilding native nations: Strategies for governance and development.* Tucson, AZ: University of Arizona Press.

Kahout, K., and Kleinfeld, J. (1974). *Alaska Natives in higher education.* Fairbanks, AK: Institute of Social and Economic Research, University of Alaska.

Kidwell, C. S. (1986). *Motivating American Indian students into graduate studies.* ERIC Digest (ED 268703).

Kidwell, C. S. (2009). American Indian Studies: Intellectual Navel Gazing or Academic Discipline? *The American Indian Quarterly, 33*(1), 1–17.

King, J. E. (1996). *Improving the odds: Factors that increase the likelihood of four-year college attendance among high school seniors. College Board Report, 96*(2). Retrieved from http://professionals.collegeboard.com/profdownload/pdf/RR%2096-2.pdf.

Kirkness, V., and Barnhardt, R. (1991). First nations and higher education: The four R's— respect, relevance, reciprocity, responsibility. *Journal of American Indian Education, 30*(3), 1–15.

Kirst, M. W., and Venezia, A. (2004). *From high school to college: Improving opportunities for success in postsecondary education.* San Francisco, CA: Jossey-Bass.

Knapp, L. G., Kelly-Reid, J. E., and Ginder, S. A. (2008). *Postsecondary Institutions in the United States: Fall 2007, Degrees and Other Awards Conferred: 2006-07, and 12-Month Enrollment: 2006-07* (NCES 2008-159). Washington, DC: National Center for Education Statistics, Institute of Education Sciences, U.S. Department of Education. Retrieved from: http://nces.ed.gov/pubsearch.

Lacourt, J. A. (2003) Descriptions of a tree outside the forest: An Indigenous woman's experiences in the academy. *The American Indian Quarterly, 27(1&2), 296–307.*

Ledlow, S. (1992, May). Is cultural discontinuity and adequate explanation for dropping out? *Journal of American Indian Education, 31*(3), 21–36.

Limb, G. (2001). Educating for practice: A profile of American Indian graduate social work students. *Journal of Ethnic and Cultural Diversity in Social Work, 10*(4), 43–62.

Lin, R. L., LaCounte, D., and Eder, J. (1988). A study of Native American students in a predominantly White college. *Journal of American Indian Education, 27*(3), 8–15.

Lintner, T. (2003). American Indian doctorate recipient 1980–2000: A quantitative and qualitative analysis. *Indigenous Nations Study Journal, 4*(1), 63–79.

Lobo, S., and Peters, K. (Eds.). (2001). *American Indians and the urban experience.* Walnut Creek, CA: Altamira Press.

Lomawaima, K. T. (2000). Tribal sovereigns: Reframing research in American Indian education. *Harvard Educational Review, 70*(1), 1–21.

Lomawaima, K. T., and McCarty, T. L. (2006). *To remain an Indian: Lessons in democracy from a century of Native American education.* New York: Teachers College Press.

Lowe, S. (2005). This is who I am: Experiences of Native American students. *New Directions for Student Services, 109,* 33–40.

Lynch, D. C. (2004). Taiwan's self-conscious nation-building project. *Asian Survey, 44*(4), 513–533.

Lyons, S. R. (2000). Rhetorical sovereignty: What do American Indians want from writing? *College Composition and Communication, 51*(3), 447–468.

Marcel, K. W. (2003). *Online advanced placement courses: Experiences of low-income and rural high school students* (pp. 1–15). Denver, CO: Western Institute Commission for Higher Education (WCALO), United States Department of Education Advanced Placement Incentive Program.

Marchbanks, R. (2011). Indian Country Fellows: Foundations pool resources to support TCU faculty dissertations, research. *Tribal College, 22*(3), 36–38, 6.

Martin, R. G. (2005). Serving American Indian students in tribal colleges: Lessons learned for mainstream colleges. In M.J.T. Fox, S. C. Lowe, and G. S. McClellan (Eds.), *New directions for student services: Serving Native American students* (pp. 79–86). San Francisco, CA: Jossey-Bass.

McAfee, M. (1997). *From their voices: American Indians in higher education and the phenomenon of stepping out* (Unpublished doctoral dissertation). Colorado State University, Fort Collins, CO.

McAfee, M. (2000). From their voices: American Indians in higher education and the phenomenon of stepping out. *Research News on Graduate Education, 2*(2), 1–10.

McCallum, M.J.L. (2009). Indigenous labor and Indigenous history. *American Indian Quarterly, 33*(4), 523–544.

McCardle, P., and Demmert, W. (2006). Improving academic performance among American Indian, Alaska Native, and Native Hawaiian students. *Journal of American Indian Education, 45*(3), 1–23.

McDonough, P. M. (1997). *Choosing colleges: How social class and schools structure opportunity.* New York: State University of New York.

McDonough, P. M. (2004). *The school–to-college transition: Challenges and prospects.* Washington, DC: American Council on Education, Center for Policy Analysis.

McDonough, P. M. (2005). Counseling matters: Knowledge, assistance, and organizational commitment in college preparation. In W. G. Tierney, Z. B. Corwin, and J. E. Colyar (Eds.), *Preparing for college: Nine elements of effective outreach* (pp. 69–88). Albany, NY: State University of New York.

McDonough, P. M., Korn, J., and Yamasaki, E. (1997). Access, equity, and the privatization of college counseling. *Review of Higher Education, 20*(3), 297–317.

McDonough, P. M., McClafferty, K. A., and Fann, A. (2002, April). *Rural college opportunity issues and challenges.* Paper presented at the Annual Meeting of the American Education Research Association, Sacramento, CA.

McNamara, P. (1982). *American Indians in higher education: A longitudinal study of progress and attainment* (Unpublished doctoral dissertation). University of California–Los Angeles, Los Angeles, CA.

Mohatt, G. V., Trimble, J., and Dickson, R. A. (2006). Psychosocial foundations of academic performance in culture based education programs for American Indian and Alaska Native youth: Reflections on a multidisciplinary perspective. *Journal of American Indian Education 45*(1), 38–59.

Moon, N. L. (2003). *Warriors: Using Rorschach and interviews to identify strengths in Indian graduate students.* Unpublished doctoral dissertation, Alliant International University.

Moran, R., and Rampey, B. (2008). *National Indian education study—Part II: The educational experiences of American Indian and Alaska native students in grades 4 and 8 (NCES 2008, 458).* Washington, DC: National Center for Education Statistics, Institute of Education Sciences, U.S. Department of Education.

National Center for Education Statistics (NCES). (1998). *Total fall enrollment in institutions of higher education and degree-granting institutions, by type and control of institution and race/ethnicity of student: 1976 to 1996.* Washington, DC: U.S. Department of Education. Retrieved February 5, 2012, from: http://nces.ed.gov/programs/digest/d98/ d98t206.asp.

National Center for Education Statistics (NCES). (2005a). *Postsecondary institutions in the United States: Fall 2003 and degrees and other awards conferred: 2002–03.* Washington, DC: U.S. Department of Education.

National Center for Education Statistics (NCES). (2005b). *Postsecondary institutions in the United States: Fall 2004 and degrees and other awards conferred: 2003–04.* Washington, DC: U.S. Department of Education.

National Center for Education Statistics (NCES). (2010). *Status and Trends in the Education of Racial and Ethnic Minorities: 2010-15.* Washington, DC: U.S. Department of Education.

National Center for Public Policy and Higher Education. (2005). *State capacity for higher education policy: A special supplement to national crosstalk: The need for state policy leadership.* Washington, DC: National Center for Public Policy and Higher Education.

National Congress of American Indians Policy Research Center. (2007). *Demographic Profile of Indian Country.* Retrieved January 30, 2012, from http://www.ncai.org/ncai/ resource/data/docs/Census_Information_Center/AI_AN_Profile_FINAL_1.11.07.pdf.

National Science Foundation (2010). *Doctorate Recipients from U.S. Universities: 2010.* Retrieved January 30, 2012, from http://www.nsf.gov/statistics/sed/data_table.cfm.

Native American Higher Education Initiative. (2005). *Capturing the dream.* Battle Creek, MI: W.K. Kellogg Foundation.

Neuerbug, L. L. (2000). *An interview of educational success among American Indian doctoral recipients* (Unpublished doctoral dissertation). Grand Forks, ND: University of North Dakota.

Nicholas, G. P. (2006). Decolonizing the archeological landscape: The practice and politics of archaeology in British Columbia. *American Indian Quarterly, 30*(3/4), 350–380.

National Indian Education Association (NIEA). (2011). *Briefing papers: 14th Annual NIEA Legislative Summit.* Washington, DC: NIEA. Retrieved from http://www.niea.org/data/ files/policy/2011lsbriefingpapers.pdf

Oakes, J. (1985). *Keeping track: How schools structure inequality.* New Haven, CT: Yale University.

Oakes, J., Rogers, J., Lipton, M., and Morrell, E. (2002). The social construction of college access: Confronting the technical, cultural, and political barriers to low-income students of color. In W. G. Tierney, and L. S. Hagedorn (Eds.), *Increasing access to college: Extending possibilities for all students* (pp. 105–122). New York: State University of New York.

Oakes, J., and Saunders, M. (2007, February). *Multiple perspectives on multiple pathways: Preparing California's youth for college, career, and civic responsibility.* Retrieved from http://www.idea.gseis.ucla.edu/publications/mp/reports/mp02.html.

Oppelt, N. T. (1990). *The tribally controlled Indian college: The beginnings of self-determination in American Indian education.* Tsaile, AZ: Navajo Community College Press.

Ortiz, A. M., and HeavyRunner, I. (2003). Student access, retention, and success: Models of inclusion and support. In M. K. Benham and W. Stein (Eds.), *The renaissance of American Indian higher education: Capturing the dream* (pp. 215–240). Mahwah, NJ: Lawrence Erlbaum.

Parker, A. C. (1916). The social elements of the Indian problem. *American Journal of Sociology, 22,* 252–267.

Patterson, D. G., Baldwin, L.-M., and Olsen, P. M. (2009). Supports and obstacles in the medical school application process for American Indians and Alaska Natives. *Journal of Health Care for the Poor and Underserved, 20*(2), 308–329.

Patterson, M. (2002). "Real" Indian songs. *American Indian Quarterly, 26*(1), 44–66.

Paulsen, M. B., and St. John, E. (2002). Social class and college costs: Examining the financial nexus between college choice and persistence. *The Journal of Higher Education, 73*(2), 189–236.

Pavel, D. M. (1998). *American Indians and Alaska natives in postsecondary education.* Washington, DC: U.S. Department of Education Office of Educational Research and Improvement National Center for Education Statistics.

Pavel, D. M. (1999). American Indians and Alaska Natives in postsecondary education: Promoting access and achievement. In K. G. Swisher and J. W. Tippeconnic (Eds.), *Next steps: Research and practice to advance Indian education* (pp. 239–258). Charleston, WV: ERIC Clearinghouse on Rural Education and Small Schools.

Pavel, D. M., and Colby, A. Y. (1992). American Indians in higher education: The community college experience. Washington, DC: Office of Educational Research and Improvement.

Pavel, D. M., and others (1998). American Indians and Alaska Natives in postsecondary education (NCES 98–291). Washington, DC: U.S. Department of Education, National Center for Education Statistics.

Pavel, M., Inglebret, E., and Banks, S. R. (2001). Tribal colleges and universities in an era of dynamic development. *Peabody Journal, 76*(1), 50–72.

Perez-Huber, L. (2009). Challenging the nativist framing: Acknowledging the community cultural wealth of undocumented Chicana college students to reform the immigration debate. *Harvard Educational Review, 79*(4), 704–784.

Perna, L.W. (2000). Differences in the decision to enroll in college among African Americans, Hispanics, and Whites. *Journal of Higher Education, 71*, 117–141.

Perna, L. W. (2005). The key to college access: Rigorous academic preparation. In W. G. Tierney, Z. B. Corwin, and J. E. Colyar (Eds.), *Preparing for college: Nine elements of effective outreach* (pp. 13–28). Albany, NY: State University of New York.

Peshkin, A. (1997). *Places of memory: Whitman's schools and Native American communities.* Mahwah, NJ: Lawrence Erlbaum.

Peterson-Hickey, M. M. (1998). *American Indian faculty experiences: Culture as a challenge and a source of strength* (Unpublished doctoral dissertation). Minneapolis, MN: University of Minnesota.

Pewewardy, C., and Frey, B. (2002). Surveying the landscape: Perceptions of multicultural support services and racial climate at a predominantly White university. *Journal of Negro Education, 71*(1/2), 77–95.

Pewewardy, C., and Frey, B. (2004). American Indian students' perceptions of racial climate, multicultural support services, and ethnic fraud at predominantly White universities. *Journal of American Indian Education, 43*(1), 32–60.

Pierce, C. M. (1995). Stress analogs of racism and sexism: Terrorism, torture, and disaster. In C. V. Willie, P. P. Rieker, B. M. Kramer, and B. S. Brown (Eds.), *Mental health, racism, and sexism* (pp. 277–293). Pittsburgh, PA: University of Pittsburgh Press.

Planty, M., Bozick, R., and Ingels, S. J. (2006). *Academic pathways, preparation, and performance: A descriptive overview of the transcripts from the high school graduating class of 2003–04 (NCES 2007, 316).* Washington, DC: National Center for Education Statistics, Institute of Education Sciences, U.S. Department of Education.

Pommersheim, F. (1984). Economic development in Indian country: What are the questions? *American Indian Law Review, 12*(2), 195–217.

Reyhner, J. (1997). The case for Native American studies. In D. Morrison (Ed.), *American Indian studies: An interdisciplinary approach to contemporary issues.* New York: Peter Lang.

Reyhner, J., Lee, H., and Gabbard, D. (1993). A specialized knowledge base for teaching American Indian students. *Tribal College, 4*(4), 26–32.

Rodriguez-Rabin, R. (2003). I left my life back South. *American Indian Quarterly, 27*(1/2), 394–399.

Rosenbaum, J. E., Deil-Amen, R., and Person, A. E. (2006). *After admission: From college access to success.* New York: Russell Sage Foundation.

Scott, W. J. (1986). Attachment to Indian culture and "difficult situation": A study of American Indian college students. *Youth and Society, 17,* 381–395.

Secatero, S. L. (2009). *Beneath our sacred minds, hands and hearts: Stories of persistence and success among American Indian graduate and professional students* (Unpublished doctoral dissertation). Albuquerque, NM: University of New Mexico.

Shield, R. W. (2004). The retention of indigenous students in higher education: Historical issues, federal policy, and indigenous resilience. *Journal of College Student Retention: Research, Theory and Practice, 6*(1), 111–127.

Shireman, R. (2004). *"Rigorous courses" and student achievement in high school.* Research report, Berkeley Center for Studies on Higher Education (CSHE.13.04). Retrieved from http://ishi.lib.berkeley.edu/cshe/

Shotton, H. (2008). *Pathway to the Ph.D.: Experiences of high-achieving American Indian females* (Unpublished doctoral dissertation). Norman OK: University of Oklahoma.

Shotton, H. J., Oosahwe, E.S.L., and Cintrón, R. (2007). Stories of success: Experiences of American Indian students in a peer-mentoring retention program. *Review of Higher Education, 31*(1), 81–108.

Shutiva, C. (2001). *Career and academic guidance for American Indian and Alaska Native youth.* ERIC Digest (EDO-RC-01–2). Eric Clearinghouse on Rural Education and Small Schools.

Smith, C., and Jackson, G. (2006). Decolonizing Indigenous archaeology: Developments from down under. *American Indian Quarterly, 30*(3/4), 311–349.

Smith, G. H. (2000). Protecting and respecting Indigenous knowledge. In M. Battiste (Ed.), *Reclaiming indigenous voice and vision*. Vancouver, Canada: UBC.

Smith, L. T. (1999). *Decolonizing methodologies: Research and indigenous peoples.* Dunedin/London, United Kingdom: University of Otago Press/Zed Books.

Smith, W. A., Hung, M., and Frankin, J. D. (2011). Racial battle fatigue and the miseducation of Black men: Racial microaggressions, societal problems, and environmental stress. *The Journal of Negro Education, 80*(1), 63–82.

Smith, W. A., Yosso, T. J., and Solórzano, D. G. (2011). Challenging racial battle fatigue on historically White campuses: A critical race examination of race-related stress. In S. R. Harper and S. Hurtado (Eds.), ASHE Reader Series, *Racial and ethnic diversity in higher education* (3rd ed., pp. 845–860). Boston, MA: Pearson Learning Solutions.

Snyder, T. D., and Dillow, S. A. (2010). *Digest of Education Statistics, 2009* (NCES 2010, 013). Washington, DC: National Center for Education Statistics, Institute of Education Sciences, U.S. Department of Education.

Solórzano, D. (1992). An exploratory analysis on the effects of race, class, and gender on student and parent mobility aspirations. *Journal of Negro Education, 61,* 30–44.

Spencer, C. (2002). Policy priorities and political realities. In D. E. Heller (Ed.), *Conditions of access: Higher education for lower-income students.* Westport, CT: American Council on Education/Preager Series on Higher Education.

Spielhagen, F. R. (2006). Closing the achievement gap in math: The long-term effects of eighth grade algebra. *Journal of Advanced Academics, 18*(1), 34–59.

Steele, C. M., and Aronson, J. (1995). Stereotype threat and the intellectual test performance of African-Americans. *Journal of Personality and Social Psychology, 69*(5), 797–811.

St. Germaine, R. (1995). *Drop-out rates among American Indian and Alaska Native students: Beyond cultural discontinuity*. Charleston, WV: ERIC Clearinghouse on Rural Education and Small Schools.

St. Germaine, R. (2008). Nation building for native youth aims to strengthen tribes. *Indian Country Today, 28*(10), 7.

St. John, E. P. (1991). What really influences minority attendance? Sequential analysis of the high school and beyond sophomore cohort. *Research in Higher Education, 32*(2), 141–158.

St. John, E. P. (2004). *Diversity and persistence in Indiana higher education: The impact of preparation, major choices, and student aid*. Bloomington, IN: Indiana Project on Academic Success: Smith Center for Research in Education.

Stage, E., and D. Hossler. (1989). Differences in family influences on college attendance plans for male and female ninth graders. *Research in Higher Education, 30,* 301–314.

Stampen, J. O., and Fenske, R. H. (1988). The impact of financial aid on ethnic minorities. *Review of Higher Education, 11*(4), 337–352.

Stanley, C. A. (2011). Coloring the academic landscape: Faculty of color breaking the silence in predominantly White colleges and universities. In S. R. Harper and S. Hurtado (Eds.), *Racial and ethnic diversity in higher education*. ASHE Reader Series (3rd ed., pp. 305–329). Boston, MA: Pearson Learning Solutions.

Stein, W. J. (1992). *Tribally controlled colleges*. New York: Peter Lang.

Stein, W. (1996). The survival of American Indian faulty. In C. Turner, M. Garcia, A. Nora, and L. Rendon (Eds.), *Racial and Ethnic Diversity in Higher Education*. ASHE Reader Series (pp. 390–397). Needham Heights, MA: Simon & Schuster Custom Publications.

Stein, W. J. (1999). Tribal colleges: 1968–1998. In K. G. Swisher and J. W. Tippeconnic (Eds.), *Next steps: Research and practice to advance Indian education* (pp. 259–270). Charleston, WV: ERIC Clearinghouse on Rural Education and Small Schools.

Stevens, E. (2002, December 17). Replacing Time magazine's falsehoods with facts. *Indian Country Today.*

Swail, W. S., and Perna, L. W. (2002). Pre-college outreach programs: A national perspective. In W. G. Tierney and L. S. Hagedorn (Eds.), *Increasing access to college: Extending possibilities for all students* (pp. 15–34). Albany, NY: State University of New York.

Swail, W. S., Redd, K. E., and Perna, L. W. (2003). *Retaining Minority Students in Higher Education: A Framework for Success*. ASHE-ERIC Higher Education Report No. 2. Washington, DC: The George Washington University, School of Education and Human Development.

Swanson, C. B. (2004). *Who graduates? Who doesn't? A statistical portrait of public high school graduation, class of 2001*. Washington, DC: The Urban Institute.

Swanson, C. B. (2009). *Cities in Crisis: Closing the Graduation Gap*. Bethesda, MD: Editorial Projects in Education Research Center. Retrieved from http://www.edweek.org/media/cities_in_crisis_2009.pdf.

Szasz, M. C. (1999). *Education and the American Indian: The road to self-determination since 1928* (3rd ed.). Albuquerque, NM: University of New Mexico.

Tribal Education Departments National Assembly (TEDNA). (2011). *Tribal Education Departments National Assembly proposed statutory language for the reauthorization of the Elementary and Secondary Education Act*. Boulder, Co: Tribal Education Departments National Assembly.

Tierney, W. (1992). *Official encouragement, institutional discouragement: Minorities in academe—The Native American experience*. Norwood, NJ: Ablex.

Tierney, W. G., and Bensimon, E. (1996). Promotion and tenure: Community and socialization in academe. Albany, NY: State University of New York Press.

Tierney, W. G., Sallee, M. W., and Venegas, K. M. (2007, Fall). Access and financial aid: How American Indian students pay for college. *Journal of College Admission, 197,* 14–23.

Tinto, V. (1975). Dropout from higher education: A theoretical synthesis of recent research. *Review of Educational Research, 45,* 89–125.

Tinto, V. (1986). Theories of student departure revisited. In J. Smart (Ed.), *Higher education: Handbook of theory and research* (Vol. II). New York: Agathon Press.

Tippeconnic, J. W. (1999). Tribal control of American Indian education: Observation since the 1960s with implications for the future. In K. G. Swisher and J. W. Tippeconnic (Eds.), *Next steps: Research and practice to advance Indian education.* Charleston, WV: ERIC Clearinghouse on Rural Education and Small Schools.

Tippeconnic, J. W. (2000). Reflecting on the past: Some important aspects of Indian education to consider as we look toward the future. *Journal of American Indian Education, 39*(2), 39–47.

Tippeconnic, J. W., and McKinney, S. (2003). Native faculty: Scholarship and development. In M.K.P. Benham and W. J. Stein (Eds.), *The renaissance of American Indian higher education, capturing the dream* (pp. 241–255). Mahwah, NJ: Lawrence Erlbaum.

Townsend, B. (1997). *Two-year colleges for women and minorities: Enabling access to the baccalaureate.* New York: Falmer.

Turner, C.S.V., Gonzalez, J. C., and Wood, J. L. (2011). Faculty of color in academe: What 20 years of literature tell us. In S. R. Harper, and S. Hurtado (Eds.), *Racial and ethnic diversity in higher education,* ASHE Reader Series (3d ed., pp. 273–304). Boston, MA: Pearson Learning Solutions.

Turner, C. V., and Meyers, S. L. (2000). *Faculty of color in academe: Bittersweet success.* Needham Heights, MA: Allyn and Bacon.

Two Bears, D. R. (2006). Navajo archaeologist is not an oxymoron: A tribal archaeologist's experience. *American Indian Quarterly, 30*(3/4), 381–387.

Umbach, P. (2011). The contribution of faculty of color to undergraduate education. In S. R. Harper and S. Hurtado (Eds.), *Racial and ethnic diversity in higher education.* ASHE Reader Series (3d ed., pp. 394–414). Boston, MA: Pearson Learning Solutions.

U.S. Commission on Civil Rights (2003). *A quiet crisis: Federal funding and unmet needs in Indian country.* Washington, DC: U.S. Commission on Civil Rights.

U.S. Department of the Interior. (2007). *GPRA strategic plan, fiscal year 2007–2012.* Washington, DC: U.S. Department of the Interior.

Vance, J. (2010). To publish or not to publish: Some faculty choose not to publish while others see advantages. *Tribal College Journal, 21*(3), 22–26.

Venegas, K. M. (2007). The Internet and college access: Challenges for low-income students. *American Academic, 3*(1), 141–154.

Villalpando, O., and Solórzano, D. (2005). The role of culture in college preparation programs: A review of the literature. In W. Tierney, Z. Corwin, and J. Kolyar (Eds.), *Preparing for college: Nine elements of effective outreach* (pp. 13–28). Albany, NY: State University of New York Press.

Villegas, M. (2009). 500 Māori PhDs in Five Years: Exploring Indigenous Community Development through Higher Education. Unpublished doctoral dissertation. Harvard University.

Voorhees, R. A. (2003). *Characteristics of Tribal College and University Faculty*. Report, American Indian College Fund. Retrieved from http://www.collegefund.org/userfiles/file/TCUFacultyPaper11.pdf

Ward, C. J. (1995). American Indian high school completion in rural southeast Montana. *Rural Sociology, 60*, 416–434.

Waterman, S. (2007). A complex path to Haudenosaunee degree completion. *Journal of American Indian Education, 46*(1), 20–40.

Watson, L., Terrell, M., Wright, D., and Associates. (2002). *How minority students experience college: Implications for planning and policy*. Hampton, VA: Stylus Publishing.

White, F. (2003). Life along the margins. *American Indian Quarterly, 27*(1/2), 441–451.

Whitt, L. A. (2004). Biocolonialism and the commodification of knowledge. In A. Waters (Ed.), *American Indian thought: Philosophical essays* (pp. 188–213). Malden, MA: Blackwell.

Wilkins, D. E. (2004). Wilkins: Indigenous voices and American politics. *Indian Country Today, 24*(11), A5.

Wilkins, D. (2001). The manipulation of Indigenous status: The federal government as shape-shifter. *Stanford Law and Policy Review, 12*(2), 223–235.

Wilkins, D. E. (2002). *American Indian politics and the American political system*. Lanham, MD: Rowman and Littlefield.

Williams, R. A. (1997). Vampires anonymous and critical race practice. *Michigan Law Review, 95*(4), 741–765.

Williamson, M. J. (1994). *Strengthening the seamless web: Fostering minority doctoral success with Mexican American and American Indian students in their doctoral programs*. Paper presented at the Annual Meeting of the American Educational research Association, New Orleans, LA, April 4–8.

Wilson, A. C. (2004). Reclaiming our humanity: Decolonization and the recovery of Indigenous knowledge. In D. A. Mihesuah and A. C. Wilson, *Indigenizing the academy: Transforming scholarship and empowering communities* (pp. 69–87). Lincoln, NE: University of Nebraska Press.

Woodcock, D., and Alawiye, O. (2001). The antecedents of failure and emerging hope: American Indians and public higher education. *Education, 121*(4), 810–820.

Woodford, B. (2005). *How to mentor graduate students*. Seattle, WA: University of Washington.

Worl, R. (1992). A Tlingit brother of Alpha Chi. In A. Garrod, and C. Larimore (Eds.), *First person, first peoples: Native American college graduates tell their life stories*. Ithaca, NY: Cornell University Press.

Wright, B. (1988). "For the children of the infidels"?: American Indian education in the colonial colleges. *American Indian Culture and Research Journal, 12*(3), 1–14.

Wright, B. (1990a). American Indian studies programs: Surviving the '80s, thriving in the '90s. *Journal of American Indian Education, 30*(1), 17–24.

Wright, B. (1990b). Tribally controlled community colleges: A student outcomes assessment of associate degree recipients. *Community College Review, 18*(3), 28–33.

Wright, B., and Tierney, W. (1991). American Indians in higher education: A history of cultural conflict. *Change, 23*(2), 11–18.

Wright, D., Hirlinger, M., and England, R. (1998). *The politics of second generation discrimination on American Indian education: Incidence, explanation, and mitigating strategies.* London, United Kingdom: Bergin and Garvey.

Yosso, T. J. (2005). Whose culture has capital? A critical race theory discussion of community cultural wealth. *Race, Ethnicity and Education, 8*(1), 69–91.

Name Index

Larimore, C., 61
Laughlin, E., 51
Ledlow, S., 44, 45
Lee, H., 45
Lee, S., 65
Limb, G., 65, 87
Lin, R. L., 60
Linn, R., 39
Lintner, T., 73
Lipton, M., 45
Lobo, S., 62
Lomawaima, K. T., 1, 16, 18
Lopez, C., 50
Lowe, S., 55
Lynch, D. C., 13
Lyons, S. R., 21
Lytle, C. M., 4, 11, 17

M
Marcel, K. W., 38
Marchbanks, R., 104
Marston, Greg, 34
Martin, R. G., 46
Maughan, E., 1
McAfee, M., 59, 60
McCallum, M.J.L., 93
McCardle, P., 34, 45
McCarty, T. L., 1, 16, 18
McClafferty, K. A., 38
McDonough, P. M., 38, 43, 45, 47, 55
McKinney, S., 92, 93, 94, 96, 101, 103, 104, 105
McNamara, P., 58
McSwain, C., 41, 43, 46, 48, 55, 65, 69
Meyers, S. L., 94, 96, 97
Mohatt, G. V., 34
Moon, N. L., 80, 82, 85, 87, 88
Moran, R., 32
Morrell, E., 45

N
National Center for Education Statistics (NCES), 8, 32, 38, 54, 56, 57, 70
National Center for Public Policy and Higher Education, 115

National Congress of American Indians Policy Research Center, 38
National Science Foundation (NSF), 74, 75, 76, 77
Native American Higher Education Initiative, 56, 70
Neuerbug, L. L., 87, 88
Nicholas, G. P., 93
National Indian Education Association (NIEA), 115

O
Oakes, J., 43, 45
Olsen, P. M., 86
Oosahwe, E.S.L., 88
Oppelt, N. T., 7, 8, 9
Ortiz, A. M., 34, 35
Oseguera, L., 55

P
Parker, A. C., 117
Pascual, F. G., 21, 22
Patterson, D. G., 86
Patterson, M., 71
Paulsen, M. B., 42
Pavel, D. M., 38, 44, 55, 58, 63, 70, 92
Pavel, M., 69
Peacock, T., 34, 44
Perez-Huber, L., 81
Perna, L., 34, 35, 40
Perna, L. W., 49, 55, 56
Person, A. E., 55
Peshkin, A., 44
Peters, K., 62
Peterson-Hickey, M. M., 95, 98, 100, 101
Pewewardy, C., 55, 65
Pierce, C. M., 84
Planty, M., 1, 35, 36
Pommersheim, F., 13
Pratt, W., 119

R
Radin, N., 45
Rampey, B., 32
Redd, K. E., 56

Subject Index

A

Academic aggression, and Indigenous students, 63

Academic concentration, 36

Academic preparation: as educational stepping stone, 59–60; and family support, 58; for higher education, 43; inadequate/poor, 45, 64, 72, 107; for postsecondary access for Indigenous students, 34–36; and student aspirations, 55

Accelerated learning opportunities, 36–39

ACT scores by race and ethnicity (2008), 40–41

AI/AN college students, 52–72; attendance, 54; campus context, 63–65; cultural differences, 60–63; enrollment patterns, 53–56; experiences in predominantly White institutions, 58–68; graduation rates, 69; paying for college, 65–68; persistence in higher education institutions, 53; retention patterns, 56–58; tribal colleges/universities, 68–71

AI/AN faculty, 91–105; as activists and advocates, 93–94; American Indian women, 95; full-time faculty in degree-granting institutions, 92; Indigenous faculty, 91–92; in mainstream colleges and universities, 91; native faculty at mainstream institutions, 95–101; role of Native faculty, 92

AI/AN graduate education, 76; doctoral-granting institutions with the largest number of AI/AN students, 76–77; doctoral recipient aspirations, 76; funding sources for Indigenous doctoral students, 76; Master's and doctoral programs, 74–76; and nation building, 88–89; research on, 73

AI/AN graduate students, 73–89; academic alienation, 78–79; academic guidance, lack of, 85–86; cultural alienation, 78–79; cultural wealth, 81; discrimination, 82–85; familial capital, 81–82; financial stressors, 86; Indigenous/professional, experience of, 77–88; Indigenous role models, lack of, 85; isolation, feelings of, 78–82; marginalization for, 77–78; racism, 82–85; support, sources of, 87–88

AI/AN higher education: historical background of, 6–9; situating in larger contexts, 3–6

Alaska Native Claims Settlement Act (ANCSA), 3

Alaska Native peoples: and Alaska Native Claims Settlement Act (ANCSA), 3; leadership, and cultural milieu of Alaska Native students, 46–47; unique status of, 3–4; use of term, 3, 4

American Indian and Alaska Natives (AI/AN), *See also specific AI/AN topics*: diverse population, 11; educational attainment, progress in, 1; as least-studied group in higher education, 9; unemployment/poverty rates for, 66

American Indian college, colonists' schemes for construction of, 6

American Indian peoples, *See also* American Indian and Alaska Natives (AI/AN); *specific AI/AN topics*: graduation from postsecondary institutions (1930s), 6–7; treaties with U.S., 4; treaty rights, 6; use of term, 3

American Indians and the Urban Experience (Lobo/Peters), 62

Andrew W. Mellon Foundation, funding for tribal college faculty, 104

Attendance, 34, 51, 59; AI/AN college students, 53–54; and cultural discontinuity, 34; and lack of funding for Indigenous students, 8

Average unmet financial need, 42

B

Barriers: to higher education, 40, 47, 52; to persistence, 64

Benefits of higher education, as viewed by Indigenous cultures, 46

Boarding-school era, 119

Bureau of Indian Affairs (BIA), 25; higher education scholarship grant program, 8

Bureau of Indian Education (BIE), 68; schools, 32

C

Casinos, 67–68

Cherokee Nation v. Georgia, 19

College counseling, 43–47

College education, and social status in tribal communities, 46

College entrance and retention rates, Indigenous students, 1

College Horizons, 50

Commonalities of experiences, of Native students and faculty, 5–6

Community survival: and indigenous knowledge systems, 16; and reciprocity, 16–17

Council of Graduate Schools, 73

Cultural differences, and AI/AN college students, 60–63

Cultural discontinuity, and Indigenous faculty, 97–100

Cultural inferiority myth, as justification for forced assimilation/acculturation of Indian people, 20

Cultural revival, 30

Cultural sovereignty, 20; as internal phenomenon, 21; and nation building, 21

Cultural wealth, 81

Culturally responsive schooling, 1, 27–28

Cumulative promotion index (CPI), 33–34

D

Dartmouth College, education of American Indian students (late 1700s), 6

Development projects, 22

Discrimination, and AI/AN graduate students, 82–85; and Indigenous faculty, 100–101

Diversity, among Indigenous peoples, 15

Dual citizenship, 11–12

E

Early-college high schools (ECHS) for Native youth, 50–51

Economic conditions, and college tuition, 40–43

Economic development, 23–27; culturally appropriate economic models, building, 25; diversity within the economy, 25–26; Hupa model of, 25–26; successful economic models, 26; of tribal lands, 25

Educational pipeline, 2

Effie Kokrine Charter High School (EKCS), Fairbanks AL, 51

Enrollment patterns, AI/AN college students, 53–56

Executive Order 13336 (2004), 6; and nation-to-nation relationships, 20

Extraconstitutionality, of sovereignty, 4

F

Familial capital, 81–82
Family education model (FEM), 59
Family income, and going to college, 42
Family involvement, 47–48
Federal aid, used to support postsecondary education, 67
Federally recognized tribes, 3, 11
Food sovereignty, 21–22
Formal education, and nation building, 30
Fort Berthold Community College (FBCC), New Town ND, 71
Free Application for Federal Student Aid (FAFSA), 39

G

GEAR UP programs, 49
General education tracks, redirection of poor/minority students to, 43
Graduation rates, AI/AN college students, 69

H

Harvard University, construction of Indian College at (1617), 6; Harvard Project on American Indian Economic Development (HPAIED), 27
Haskell Indian Nations University, 104
Henrico (VA) "college for Children of the Infidels" (1617), 6
High school dropout rates, Indigenous students, 1
Higher education: academic preparation for, 43; benefits of, as viewed by Indigenous cultures, 46
Historical background, of American Indian and Alaska Native higher education, 6–9
Homelands, *See* Tribal lands
House Concurrent Resolution (HCR) 108 (1953), 4
Hupa model of economic development, 25–26

I

Indian gaming, 67–68
Indian Self-Determination and Education Assistance Act (U.S. Public Law 95-638), 14
Indigenous faculty, 91, 91–92; cultural discontinuity, 97–100; discrimination, 100–101; institutional support, lack of, 97–100; isolation and lack of encouragement for research interests, 95–97; mentorship, lack of, 97–100; and nation building, 94–95; racism, 100–101; tokenizing of, 101; in tribal colleges and universities, 101–103
Indigenous knowledge systems, 1, 15–17, 60; and community survival, 16, 16–17; systematic nature of, 15–16
Indigenous peoples: diversity among, 15; repatriation process, 20–21; unique histories of, 6; use of term, 3–5
Indigenous students: and academic aggression, 63; college entrance and retention rates, 1; college preparatory courses, completion of, 1; high school dropout rates, 1; institutions of higher education, 1–3; postsecondary access for, 31–52; and pursuit of postsecondary education, reasons for, 2; scholarships for, 1930s compared to 1960s, 7, 9
Institutional practice, discussion/implications for, 116–117
Investors, in tribal future, defined, 26

J

Job stability, and tribal-specific and/or tribally controlled economic enterprises, 25
Jobs: in Indian gaming, 25, 68; lack of, 24, 52; on tribal lands, 71
Justice-oriented notion of nation building (Blain), 23

K

Kellogg Foundation, 70
Klamath Early College High School of the Redwoods (Yurok Reservation, CA), 51

L

Land claims: Alaska Native peoples, 3; American Indian peoples, 4–6, 15

About the Authors

Bryan McKinley Jones Brayboy (Lumbee) is Borderlands Associate Professor of Indigenous Education, codirector of the Center for Indian Education, and coeditor of the *Journal of American Indian Education* at Arizona State University and President's Professor of Indigenous Education at University of Alaska–Fairbanks. His research focuses on the experiences of Indigenous students and the intersections between race, law, and education.

Amy J. Fann is an assistant professor in the Counseling and Higher Education Program at the University of North Texas. Her research focuses on postsecondary access, including parental involvement in college preparation and planning, the work of tribal education departments and programs in getting American Indian students into and through college, and the role of higher education in Native nation building and economic development.

Angelina E. Castagno is an assistant professor of Educational Leadership and Foundations at Northern Arizona University. Her teaching and research centers around issues of equity and diversity in U.S. schools, and she is especially interested in issues of race, whiteness, and Indigenous education. Her publications include articles in *Anthropology and Education Quarterly*, *Race and Ethnicity in Education,* and the *Review of Educational Research.*

Jessica A. Solyom is a doctoral student in the Department of Justice & Social Inquiry at Arizona State University. Her research interests focus on Indigenous justice and American Indian student activism; Latina/Latino immigration, education and human/civil rights struggles; and the intersection of race, gender, and class in the fashion and beauty industry. Her scholarship has appeared in the *Nevada Law Journal,* and she has coauthored book chapters that address teaching and conducting research in urban educational settings as well as critical Indigenous research methodologies. She is currently working on two articles on the topic of Indigenous justice and an article that focuses on immigration law in Arizona.

About the ASHE Higher Education Report Series

Since 1983, the ASHE (formerly ASHE-ERIC) Higher Education Report Series has been providing researchers, scholars, and practitioners with timely and substantive information on the critical issues facing higher education. Each monograph presents a definitive analysis of a higher education problem or issue, based on a thorough synthesis of significant literature and institutional experiences. Topics range from planning to diversity and multiculturalism, to performance indicators, to curricular innovations. The mission of the Series is to link the best of higher education research and practice to inform decision making and policy. The reports connect conventional wisdom with research and are designed to help busy individuals keep up with the higher education literature. Authors are scholars and practitioners in the academic community. Each report includes an executive summary, review of the pertinent literature, descriptions of effective educational practices, and a summary of key issues to keep in mind to improve educational policies and practice.

The Series is one of the most peer reviewed in higher education. A National Advisory Board made up of ASHE members reviews proposals. A National Review Board of ASHE scholars and practitioners reviews completed manuscripts. Six monographs are published each year and they are approximately 144 pages in length. The reports are widely disseminated through Jossey-Bass and John Wiley & Sons, and they are available online to subscribing institutions through Wiley Online Library (http://wileyonlinelibrary.com).

Call for Proposals

The ASHE Higher Education Report Series is actively looking for proposals. We encourage you to contact one of the editors, Dr. Kelly Ward (kaward@wsu.edu) or Dr. Lisa Wolf-Wendel (lwolf@ku.edu), with your ideas.

Recent Titles

ASHE HIGHER EDUCATION REPORT

ORDER FORM SUBSCRIPTION AND SINGLE ISSUES

DISCOUNTED BACK ISSUES:

Use this form to receive 20% off all back issues of *ASHE Higher Education Report*.
All single issues priced at **$23.20** (normally $29.00)

TITLE   ISSUE NO.   ISBN

_____ _____ _____

_____ _____ _____

_____ _____ _____

Call 888-378-2537 or see mailing instructions below. When calling, mention the promotional code JBNND to receive your discount. For a complete list of issues, please visit www.josseybass.com/go/aehe

SUBSCRIPTIONS: (1 YEAR, 6 ISSUES)

☐ New Order   ☐ Renewal

U.S.	☐ Individual: $174	☐ Institutional: $281
CANADA/MEXICO	☐ Individual: $174	☐ Institutional: $341
ALL OTHERS	☐ Individual: $210	☐ Institutional: $392

Call 888-378-2537 or see mailing and pricing instructions below.
Online subscriptions are available at www.onlinelibrary.wiley.com

ORDER TOTALS:

Issue / Subscription Amount: $ _____

Shipping Amount: $ _____
(for single issues only – subscription prices include shipping)

Total Amount: $ _____

SHIPPING CHARGES:
First Item $6.00
Each Add'l Item $2.00

(No sales tax for U.S. subscriptions. Canadian residents, add GST for subscription orders. Individual rate subscriptions must be paid by personal check or credit card. Individual rate subscriptions may not be resold as library copies.)

BILLING & SHIPPING INFORMATION:

☐ **PAYMENT ENCLOSED:** *(U.S. check or money order only. All payments must be in U.S. dollars.)*

☐ **CREDIT CARD:** ☐ VISA ☐ MC ☐ AMEX

Card number _____ Exp. Date _____

Card Holder Name _____ Card Issue # _____

Signature _____ Day Phone _____

☐ **BILL ME:** *(U.S. institutional orders only. Purchase order required.)*

Purchase order # _____
Federal Tax ID 13559302 • GST 89102-8052

Name _____

Address _____

Phone _____ E-mail _____

Copy or detach page and send to: **John Wiley & Sons, One Montgomery Street, Suite 1200, San Francisco, CA 94104-4594**

Order Form can also be faxed to: **888-481-2665**

PROMO JBNND